I Married the Military

The Roots of My Life

By Jessica M. Brewer

Copyright © 2020. By Jessica M. Brewer
ISBN: 978-1-7354477-0-4

All rights reserved. No portion of this document may be reproduced in any form without expressed, written consent from the author. I have tried to recreate events, locales and conversations from my memories of them. In order to maintain their anonymity in some instances I have changed the names of individuals and places, I may have changed some identifying characteristics and details such as physical properties, occupations and places of residence. This book was self-published with the help of BusyB Writing, LLC.

DEDICATION

This book is dedicated to my parents, Ronald H. Rainess Sr. and Joanne M. Rainess. They have been my inspiration from the day I was born. Without them guiding me through life and helping me become the person I am today, I'm not sure what path I would have taken. I am proud to call them my parents because they have supported me throughout my ups and downs. Thank you for supporting and continuing to support my Army Family. I could never repay you both for all the love and support you have shown. I never had the chance to tell you how much you mean to me. I love you to the moon and back! No matter where the Army send us and the miles that stand in between, you both will always stay close to my heart.

        Love always and forever,

            Dipper

GEORGE,
Thank you so much for your support. Please check out my website and stay in touch!
www.JessicaMBrewer.com

JMB

ACKNOWLEDGMENTS

There are no words that I can ever say to express my gratitude and love towards all the amazing people that I am surrounded by. Each and everyone in my life, whether you are family, friends, or acquaintance, has not only encouraged me, but I have learned from you. Whether it was your attitude, kindness, loving, selflessness, opinions, or even your thoughtfulness, I am blessed that throughout my life, I have gained a piece to my puzzle from all of you. It would be near impossible to accomplish such an incredible book of "The Roots of My Life" without you all.

To My Daughter: Jaylynn, since the day you were born, I made a promise to myself that I would do everything in my power to be the best mother to you. I know life definitely threw me some curveballs at times, but you gave me the power to keep trying and to never give up. I have learned the most from you. You made me a mom, and I could never thank you enough for changing my life and giving me everything I never thought I could. You were my first baby, and I am proud of the beautiful woman you have become. I will always support you and your dreams because you made my dream come true. I love you always and forever.

To My Husband: Casey W. Brewer. You have been my rock since the day I met you. I could never imagine living this life without you. Your sensitivity and gentle hugs have surrounded our family to be united as one, making us all feel complete. You have supported me throughout my journey just as much as I supported you. I could never love you any more than I do today because my love for you goes beyond life itself. When I say I love you more, I am saying that no matter what obstacle we may face, we will always do it together. I can honestly say that we are a great team together for better or for worse. I have your 6.

To my Sister: Shannon M. Priest. Growing up with you made the best memories of all. I loved playing outside in the snow with you as we are making tunnels out of the big snowbanks dad used to make for us. I can remember after playing for hours, we'd sit at the kitchen table drinking hot chocolate together. Christmas was my favorite holiday with you, and that's why I still love Christmas so much today—not to mention spending time at camp. We were always on an adventure together. You will always be my best friend and loving sister. I cherish those memories we shared together as siblings. No matter how many miles are distancing us apart, you will always be my sister. Love you!

To my Grandma: Lois Rainess. God gave me a blessing to have such a loving grandma in my life. I hope you know how much I love and adore you. With the few memories that I have of you and Grandpa together, I treasure them each and every day. When I was a child, I can remember being at Uncle Wayne's farmhouse running around without a care in the world. Now, it fills my heart with more love and compassion for others. I hope Grandpa, Aunt Dolly, and our family's angels are looking down upon us to see how close we have become and always will be. Love you, Grandma, you will always have a piece of my heart.

To My Grandparents: John Klock, Jr. and Catherine Klock. Most of my memories are at Rosewood Circle in North Syracuse. I can remember Grandpa playing the Alvin and the Chipmunk Christmas song that we all loved. Going up and down the stairs ringing that bell until Grandpa told us no more. Remember Grandpa's antique peanut contraption that you pull out and the peanuts fall into your hand? I loved that thing. Grandma always wearing her favorite Santa Sweater sitting in the corner at the bar. Her clams casino dip is still amazing. Thank you for making so many memories with me. You both have given me so much to be grateful for. You both carry a puzzle piece to my heart that makes my childhood complete. Love you always. Hugs!

To my Publisher: Bianca Scott. You have made my dream come true. I could never thank you enough for inspiring me to be a great author. You have shown me how to write my emotions and have taught me so much within this journey. I know that I have more to learn from the great teacher you are. Not only are you my publisher, but you're my friend too. At times I feel that we have known each other forever because it seems natural to talk to you on a personal level. Thank you for holding my hand and showing me the path to success. P.S. Thank you for your kindness and for sacrificing your time for my dreams.

INTRODUCTION

My name is Jessica (Rainess) Brewer, and I was born in Syracuse, New York, at Crouse Hospital on February 5th. My parents were both born in the city as well and grew up together on Gale Ave. They were high school sweethearts in the 1960s. Later, we migrated to a little town called Parish, New York. This is a place where everybody knows everybody, and if you didn't know them, they sure knew you. My parents are my rock, and I couldn't imagine my life without them.

When I was a little baby, my parents nicknamed me Dipper. They both said that I would never sleep when I was a baby and that I had to be the center of attention when my parents would have their friends over. They said my sister always went to bed when they laid her down but not me. I was always up with the stars.

Since I mentioned her, now is the time to bring up my siblings. Like I just alluded to a moment ago, I have an older sister, Shannon, who I love to pieces and an older brother, Ronnie, I hardly know. It's not because I choose to; it's just that he doesn't come around often. People are always shocked when they find out I have a brother. In truth, I guess I am too because we all never see or hear from him, but that's his choice, not ours. My sister has three beautiful daughters and one handsome son. She started her adult life much sooner than I and was blessed with two granddaughters from her oldest daughter.

My brother has one beautiful daughter and two handsome sons. He also had a son named Anthony, who was tragically taken from us due to SIDS. My brother is the oldest of my parents' three children. He is also a grandfather to a sweet young boy and a little baby girl by his oldest daughter.

Now that you know a little about my siblings, let's get back to me and my childhood. I grew up on a dirt road called Hong Kong. I was always curious about who named the road. Everybody looks at me like I was from a foreign country at times when they heard the name of the road that I lived on. It was a safe road that was seldom traveled, and there were very few houses. I can still remember our neighbor, Mr. Piper. He was a grumpy old man, and everyone was intimidated by him. He used to work as a store clerk when Ezze Truck Stop was first built. Dear heavens, don't make him mad because he will be at your doorstep in *no* time. He had a deep, raspy voice that would scare the pants off of you if you heard him yell.

Apart from Mr. Piper, we had some great neighbors. Caddy-corner to our house was Tom and Betty Burke, who were the nicest couple you'd ever meet. On the other side of our house lived another lady named Mrs. Caswell. I loved her so much because she always welcomed me into her home with open arms. Further down the road is Bristol's Farm. I spent many summers with my mom's friend Sue at a 4-H recreational program and her daughter's Jaqi and Jeni. We used to grow vegetables, sew our own clothes, and then bring them to the Oswego County Fair for a contest. Sue inspired me when I was younger, showing me that I can do anything I wanted as long as I put my mind to it.

In June of 1997, I graduated from Altmar-Parish-Williamstown High School. I loved school, but only because of the sports in which I was remotely involved. I wasn't a straight "A" student, but I was damn close. I made it on the Honor Roll list on multiple occasions and the President's List one time, so I definitely had a feel for academics.

After graduating from APW High School, I was accepted into Jefferson Community College's Paralegal program. This opened many new doors by meeting different people and gaining new friendships. Come to find out, some friends were army soldiers from Fort Drum. Back then, I didn't know much about the army. All I knew was that it was great to know them when I would be invited to study groups, bowling, and parties. Before I realized it, I was making more and more friends in college.

At this point in my life, I was independent—paying my own bills and working at Fat Nancy's Tackle shop to support myself. I went to school all day then worked from 4 p.m. to 9 p.m. I loved working for Mike and Rob. They were great bosses to me. If we were slow and I'd gotten all my work done early, they would let me do my homework in their office.

My nickname was "Thinker" because I always was very thoughtful and inquisitive. It was a play off of the fishing term Hook Line and Sinker. Since they knew I loved to fish and I was always full of knowledge, the nickname Thinker was born. Between you and me, I think I was their favorite employee too. At times, the two would love to pick on me, but I didn't mind because we all laughed about it later.

When I would come into work, Mike and Rob would ask me if I learned anything today. I would always reply, "No," just joking around. They would say to me that the only thing I needed to know was that, "There is no business like show business." Our conversations were quite entertaining, to say the least.

We were so close that I used to wrap Mike and Rob's Christmas presents back then so their kids wouldn't see them. I enjoyed doing that. I would also watch Rob's kids from time to time. He had three kids, and each one had their own little personalities. Gabrielle was so sweet and precious, but her brothers, Ryan and Reese, were two peas in a pod. Overall, they were great kids. I adored the kids because they were so well behaved.

***

During my college years, I experienced unexpected deaths of friends and loved ones. I never thought I would ever experience such sadness in my life. With all the ups and downs I went through, I realize now that some years weren't so bad after all.

At the age of 25, I gave birth to a sweet baby girl in February 2004. I spent eight years as a single mother. Yeah...that was tough. The sacrifices are only known by mothers who have lived that life. I met my amazing husband on August 22, 2013, and we were married on October 23, 2013, right before he deployed. This is when my life changed, and you will soon learn why. This marked the beginning of the roots of my life story and how I was able to overcome all obstacles that came my way.

MY YOUNGER YEARS

Before I was born, my parents lived in Lakeport, New York. This was before they bought the house in Parish located on the infamous Hong Kong Road. It was out in the middle of the country. Their neighbors were far and in between, and Hong Kong Road remained a dirt road for several years. Our house was made of lath and newspaper for insulation, which made it interesting because most houses are made of sheet-rock. In case you didn't know, lath is little thin strips of wood that are used to form a foundation to the wall.

Due to how the house was built, as we grew up, we would find different objects hidden in the walls of the house. I can recall the time my mother told me that they had found a pair of baby shoes and a picture of a young woman in the wall in our living room. Can you believe that? A pair of baby shoes!

At one point during my childhood, my mother swore that the house was haunted. I can remember my mother telling Shannon and me a story of when Shannon was a baby. Before I was born, my mom said that she laid my sister down in the crib upstairs. Both my room and my sister's room are directly across from each other. We literally can open both of our doors and look into each other's rooms. Her room was in the back of the house, and mine was in the front of the house overlooking the big flowering tree.

In the back of the house, you can see outside where my parents had a huge fire pit and always had bonfires. Well, after my mom laid my sister down to sleep, she went outside to the bonfire with their friends. Mom happened to look up at the window to Shannon's room and saw a man and a woman standing in front of the window. Mom looked around and noticed that everyone was outside, and no one should have been inside the house. She went into the house and went upstairs, and no one was there in Shannon's room. But what she did notice is that all the stuffed animals were in her crib, and Shannon was pushed up into the corner.

My mom asked if anyone was upstairs in Shannon's room, and everyone responded, "No."

"Why?" asked my dad.

"I first saw a man and a woman in Shannon's window, and I went up to check on her, and all her stuffed animals were in her crib. Nobody was up there," my mom said slowly. They both just looked at each other in shock. Regardless, they went on with their night. But the weirdness didn't stop there.

My mother's cousins were watching my sister and

me one evening, and they saw a mist that resembled a gloomy cloud slowly moving up and down the stairs. They said that they felt the most uncomfortable, cold feeling they had ever experienced. My mother said her cousins would never come watch us at our house again. They told her that it made them jump out of their skin.

My mother said that she believes something happened to the woman's child because she felt like she was trying to protect us kids from something. My mother also found a pipe and an old carousel in the wall as well. She thinks that either the woman's husband or her father did something bad, or the woman tried to protect her child in some way. My mother was always scared of remodeling the house or digging into the ground to set a foundation, thinking that someday they would find human remains. As of the writing of this book, they never have.

***

While my father worked very hard to fix up the house, my mom was undecided on what she wanted the final design to be. The house needed so many repairs. She still tells me to this day that she hates the house, and she never wanted to buy it in the first place.

As I reflect on my childhood, I cannot help but recall all the blood, sweat, and tears my father poured into that house to make it bigger and better for his family. My father remodeled the house so many times throughout the years I can't even count on both hands. We had this beautiful tree in the front yard by my bedroom window which would always bloom around the Fourth of July.

Sadly, none of us know the name of this beautiful tree because nobody has ever seen anything like it. While I cannot tell you the name of the tree, I can tell you that this tree is at the root of my childhood memories. My dad wanted to cut it down so many times, but my mother said no. They were working on the front porch and had ideas to expand the house to make it more spacious, but the tree was there. Mom thought it was too beautiful to cut down, plus it provided shade during the summer months.

I remember very well how small our house was when my parents purchased our home. I can recall having a front enclosed porch right off of the living room; it was so small that there was not even enough room to walk through.

I can remember standing on the porch watching my sister, Shannon, get on the bus. I was fearless and determined that one day I was going to get on the bus with her and go to school. I envied her for being a big sister and always wanted to be by her side. Every afternoon, I used to stare out the window waiting for her to get off the bus. She was my comfort zone back then, and I looked up to her. I could not wait until the day I started school. I would think to myself, *It is going to be the best day ever getting on that bus with her.*

***

Altmar Elementary School was the best. Mr. Hudson was a great principal, and I will never forget him. He cared about all of the children that attended his school. I remember Mr. Hudson fondly, but what I remember most about him is his sense of humor. He used to make us kids laugh all the time. Once he met me and shook my hand, he remembered my last name and related me to my sister, Shannon. I never could understand how he remembered all the kid's names over the years when he was principal. Today, I can't even call both of my boys by their birth names. I am still confused at the age of 40.

He had a secretary named Mrs. Bernard, and she was a really a sweet woman. She always had a smile on her face when you walked into the office. Her children went to school at Altmar-Parish-Williamstown as well, but they graduated from high school and were already in college. I thought it was amazing that her son played football for Syracuse University. All of us kids thought it was the coolest thing. Her son would come into our class as a substitute teacher for our physical education class. It was like we all wanted to grow up and be just like him because, as a kid, most of us grew up as huge Syracuse University fans.

I remember we used to have fundraisers for the school. We would sell a variety of items like wrapping paper, candy, or Little Caesar's pizza. Every time I sold something, I had the same routine. I used to go to Tom and Betty Burke's house, and Betty always bought something from me no matter what. One day Mrs. Burke, she was so sweet, went in for hip surgery and passed away due to complications from a blood clot. We were all saddened by her unexpected death.

Then there was Mrs. Caswell. She, too, would always buy something from me every year. She was often alone after the passing of her husband, so she loved my company. She would always have hot chocolate and a snack ready for me when I arrived. I didn't have to sell anything to go see her.

I just went because I wanted to. She always called me "Dear" and told me stories about when her and her husband first moved into their farmhouse down the road from us. She said, "This house was built in the 1800s, and it was a dirt road for many of years. We didn't have any neighbors, really. It was quiet and peaceful." I was always fascinated by listening to her memories and her life. But I believe she enjoyed telling us her history. It was a great experience.

Overall, our childhood was very simple. I know we didn't have a perfect childhood, but what child does? Unless you are raised by a rich family who gives you everything that you need and desire, life isn't always easy. Even though my sister and I didn't have *exactly* everything we wanted or desired, I knew we were rich in love.

My parents weren't exactly wealthy, but they both tried to be great supporting parents. They, too, had to fight the demons and the skeletons in their closets. Parenting skills just don't come naturally; it's called trial and error. It's not like they hand out a manual when you become parents.

Being aware of faults and mistakes, I am sure many parents would go back in time and do things differently. I completely understand that desire. The desire to go back in time and avoid all the mistakes of your past. I especially understood it once I gave birth to my first child. Sure, some things could have been avoided, but later in life, I realized that there would be a lot of things that were inevitable.

***

My parents did what they could to make our childhood the best and leave us with great memories. One of my fondest childhood memories was camping on the St. Lawrence River. It is one of the best memories I have as a child with my family. My mother's parents would rent a so-called camp that actually looked like a house right on the St. Lawrence River. I loved the fact that when you walked out the front door, you can actually see Brockville, Canada, directly across the water. It was so pretty at night because you would be sitting in the screened-in porch and watch Brockville light up at dusk.

From time to time, my sister and I would get to see the different cargo ships that would sail on the Canadian side. Grandpa Klock would let us see the ships up close with his binoculars. At camp, we also had a boat dock that lead into the water in which my sister and I would fish from every day. When we weren't fishing, my grandmother Catherine Klock would teach Shannon and I how to knit and crochet.

On Friday, my mother would pack all our bags to get ready to travel that evening. When Dad came home from work at 5:30 p.m., the van would be packed, he would change his clothes, and off we all went. It was only a two-hour drive. We couldn't wait to get to camp, get unpacked, and head to the fishing dock. Especially me; I would be sitting on the dock with my fishing pole and a styrofoam container full of worms ready to hook bass or perch in the rain. I loved bass fishing, especially hooking one in the mouth! The fish would jump out of the water, and the adrenaline rush would have me pumping with excitement.

My Grandpa, John Klock, Jr., would let my parents take my sister and I out on the boat to fish on the river. We would use the fish depth finder to locate all the great fishing spots. I used to love hearing it beep when small schools of fish would pass under the boat. I was always on the edge of my seat, hoping to see the tip of my pole bend down to let me know I got a bite.

I remember when I would get a bite, the fishing line took off in the other direction. One morning, my mom and dad took my sister and me out on the boat. I can remember getting a bite, and my pole bent over the boat, ready to snap.

My mom said, "Look, Dipper, you got a bite! Pick up your pole really quick to set the hook."

So, I picked it up and yanked backwards. "I think I got it! I think I got it!" I screamed excitedly.

My dad was helping me grip the pole, so it didn't get lost overboard. "Keep reeling, Dipper," he said confidently. "You got it."

I was feeling ecstatic that I had finally caught a huge fish. As I was reeling the fish in, I saw the teeth of a pike that bit and snapped my line before my dad could get his knife out to cut it. It was a scary moment for me. It seriously took fishing to another level, which made me scared of catching a bigger fish like that. But now you go fishing, and it seems like everything has been pumped up on steroids because they are so big.

I caught a pike on another occasion too. I was at my Aunt Francis and Uncle Walt's camp. Off of their dock, the water was deeper than at our camp, and we always caught different types of fish there: sunfish, perch, bass, and rock bass. I didn't like catching eels or carp. I was always told to cut my line if we caught either of them, especially pike because they are not good for eating.

This day, I was doing my usual thing, when the line snapped. I had one! With fishing, there is always an element of surprise, and I was eager to get my line in to see what I had caught. To my surprise, it was another pike. All I could see is the pike's teeth again. I quickly realized that it had swallowed the hook, and the fish was not going to snap the line this time. I screamed so loud that my parents probably thought I fell in the water and was drowning. My father came running down the stairs to the dock to cut my line. I was so scared, and despite my love of swimming, I wouldn't even go swimming off of their dock anymore.

As a child, my parents knew that I was adventurous and full of surprises. I wasn't scared of anything when I was little unless I believed that it could actually hurt me. I can remember trying to cast my line out into the water, and my sister yells, "Ouch! Jessica got me again!"

I literally went to cast my line and the hook would get caught in her hair or snag her jacket. That's when my Dad said, "Let me do that for you because I don't need anyone to get a hook in the eye!"

I would just chuckle. I didn't do it intentionally, but it was funny. My sister had the most luck with Dad casting her line out that day because she caught a nice bass. My sister held the bass record in the family—it was a 16-incher. It was cool seeing the bass jumping out of the water like a dolphin. She was so proud the day she caught it, but she almost went water skiing just to get it reeled in. My parents had to help her because she would have gone overboard.

"Let me help you!" my Dad screamed as Shannon kept getting more and more exhausted. The bass put up a huge fight, and it was the most exciting catch that I witnessed. Through my childhood eyes, that fish was humongous, and we were happy to eat it.

Bass fishing was my favorite. I used to sit on the edge of our dock for hours. One day, I was fishing, and it started to sprinkle. My mother came out just as I was reeling in my first bass to tell me, "Honey, it's time to get up to camp. It looks like it's going to rain."

"I want to stay for a little bit longer!" I whined. Instead of fighting with me, she sat down by my side while I kept hooking one bass after another. After a while, it started to rain heavier. It was so amazing to see these fish come to the surface to eat while it was raining, and I couldn't keep them off my hook. My mother continued to sit with me in the rain, amazed at how we had never witnessed anything like this.

After the rain began to pour down, she said, "Let's hurry up and get to camp."

"Ok!" I agreed as I ran up to camp with my worms. We were regaling my grandparents with how the bass were jumping. We didn't know that they had witnessed the fish jump out of the water from the screened-in porch. They agreed that they had never seen a sight like it before. But that was not the last interesting event that happened at camp.

I can say that I almost gave my mother a heart attack one day. I was trying to build a tree fort with my dad's tools. As I was screwing into a board, I happened to drill the screw into my leg near my knee. I didn't realize that the screw had went straight through the board into my flesh. When I got done screwing the board, I must have ripped the screw out of my leg as I stood up to screw it into the other board. Crazy thing is I didn't feel it happen.

When I stood up and saw all the blood gushing down my leg, I had realized what I had done. My sister Shannon started freaking out. "Mom and Dad! Help! Jessica is bleeding!" she screamed.

When she reached me and saw what had happened, my mother was frantic. "What was she doing?" she asked Shannon.

"She was using Dad's screw gun to build the fort!"

I remember Mom carrying me into the kitchen, yelling for Grandma Klock. "Mom, can you get me an old towel or something to help stop the bleeding?" she asked Grandma Klock. As my mother and grandma were trying to get the wound to clot, my mother and grandmother were talking back and forth.

"I think she may need stitches!" said Mom anxiously.

"Well, let's see if we can stop the bleeding first and see how deep it is before we make that drive," said my grandma.

"Let's just take her just in case she needs a tetanus shot," chimed in Dad.

"Both girls are up to date on their shots," said Mom abruptly, "but that is not what I am worried about." My mother was worried if it was deep enough to need stitches. They would have had to drive an hour or more to get me to the hospital emergency room. My mom was monitoring the bleeding, and it started to coagulate after a while.

"Well, geez," my Mom said to me later. "With the amount of blood you lost, you would have thought it was much worse."

"I thought it was wider than it initially looked," said Dad.

"It is deep, but I think that it will be ok," concluded Mom. They felt that they could bandage it up so I wouldn't need to go get stitches. Needless to say, I still have a little war scar on my knee to remember that lovely day.

***

Every year, we were excited for summer because it was the one special time that our family was able to see my Uncle Walt and Aunt Fran. They lived in Florida for most of the year and came to New York to spend summers on the river. Uncle Walt is my grandfather's brother. He and Grandpa had a love for nature, which I extremely respected. I loved hearing their passion for fishing.

They used to tell us all the stories about their adventures of fishing in different lakes, ponds, rivers, streams, and in the ocean. Cousin Wally would bring his boat up and dock it at Uncle Walt's and Aunt Fran's camp—Cousin Wally and Cousin Danny's parents. I always stayed stuck to my Cousin Dan's hip. Dan is my second cousin, my mother's first.

I remember his wife, Charlotte, who was an inspiration to me while growing up because she was so smart and knowledgeable. I thoroughly enjoyed listening to her adventures, and I thought to myself that someday, I would be just like her. I loved Cousin Dan and Charlotte's little baby, Emma. I remember her sitting in her bouncy seat, kicking her feet so much that she would rock herself to sleep. She would smile and laugh all the time; she was a happy baby.

I was always inspired by how Cousin Dan and Charlotte traveled across the globe. I enjoyed listening to them tell their stories about different cultures. I can remember when they visited Czechoslovakia and brought back two letters, one for my sister Shannon and one for me. Cousin Dan set both of us up with pen pals. I was so excited to open it and start writing to her immediately.

Of course, because we were both young, it really didn't last long. The writing back and forth got a little boring, but it was a great experience to learn from someone in another country. I was fascinated with their culture. I was always envious that they were able to experience different cultures by traveling the world, and our family was not. I couldn't wait to grow up to have my own adventures.

Another reason why I loved camp was because it was closer to my Dad's family who lived in Canton, New York. My grandfather had passed due to Parkinson's Disease when I was little. I wish I had more memories of him. Uncle Wayne, who is my grandmother's brother, lives in the farm house where my dad grew up.

My Grandma Rainess lives in an apartment. My Uncle Wayne's wife Dolly had passed recently, but I always loved to see my father's family when I had the chance. My Grandma Rainess and I are very close. She holds a special place in my heart. We talk as much as we can, and I send her pictures of the kids all the time. I want her to know how much she is loved, and I want her to see my children grow. It's hard not knowing when the next time I may see her again considering the miles that stand between us.

Looking back at my upbringing as an adult, I realize my childhood was quite simple. It was enriched with being outside and playing with what nature had to offer, riding bikes, and catching fireflies. As a child, I used to ride my bicycle to my friend Barb's house, which was located catty-corner from Hong Kong Road on Route 104. Barb lived in a beautiful log cabin, which was always decorated so sophisticatedly.

My other friend Jamie lived right next to Barb, and state land was in between both of their houses. Jamie and I went to the same pre-school in Mapleview in which Tom Cutuli's mother was my teacher. My mom and dad were very good friends with Tom for many years until he passed. Tom Cutuli's family-owned and operated grocery store called the IGA was located next to their residence and the preschool. It was very easy and convenient back then.

Barb and I met through Jamie because she used to watch Jamie and her brother Joe for Joanne and

Loren. Barb used to watch us over at Jamie's house when Joanne and Loren worked late during the summers. We used to go to state land to have our adventures. State land is a piece of property that the state employees use to store dirt, paving equipment, or even draining pipes for roads.

We used to go over there and climb the dirt mounds and play house in the cylinders. There were always wasp nests in the cylinders, but we still played until they started to attack us.

We would also go over to Jamie's house and roller skate in her basement. I always had a blast at her house roller skating. That was the "in" thing back then. Almost every Friday night, we would go to Pulaski and skate at the roller-skating rink. It was always something to look forward to for the weekend until one day it burnt to the ground. Jamie and I would continue to roller skate at her house. If I'm being truthful, I was a little jealous of Jamie because her parents would give her everything she wanted back then.

We both liked the New Kids on the Block, which was a popular boy band back in that era. Jamie's room was completely decorated with the boy band's paraphernalia. She had curtains, bedding, and all the New Kids on the Block posters. She had things that I couldn't even imagine having in my life. If I received even one present for Christmas with the boy band on it, I was ecstatic. My favorite band member was Jordan. I just loved him and couldn't wait for a chance to finally see them in concert.

One day, my childhood friends Billie Jo and David asked me to go to the concert with them. Their mother Linda bought us tickets and took us to the Carrier Dome to see The New Kids on the Block. I was about 10 years old, and I thought I was in love! It was a great time, and I will never forget it.

It was my first concert, and the experience was wild. Everyone was screaming their names and crying at the same time because it was *their* boy crush. I looked over and saw these girls crying uncontrollably, thinking to myself, *Do these girls know that Jordan and Joey will never be their boyfriends? Like, give it a break, girls!* It was the most bipolar reactions you would have ever seen. I was just excited to see them in person and not on a poster. The jumbo screen was really cool to see them up close. The lights and lasers were super cool and gave me whiplash. There was so much that caught the eye like everyone's glow bracelets and necklaces. Just to see the live show was spectacular.

After that, Billie Jo and I would always get together to sing and dance to New Kids on the Block. Sometimes their father would bring them over to our house on a Friday or Saturday so we could play. I remember one night was mind-blowing beyond belief. My sister and I were swimming and catching fireflies with Billie Jo and David. We were begging and begging my mother and father to let them stay the night and camp out in the tent.

"Can Billie Jo and David stay the night with us?" I pleaded.

"Not tonight. Now go play," said Mom.

I went to Dad next. "Dad, Can Billie Jo and David spend the night with us?"

"Go ask your mother!" he yelled.

"She said no, but I was hoping you would say YES! We still want to play!"

"Then I guess the answer is no," he smirked.

Shannon and I were still bound and determined that night to get them to say yes. Both my mother and their father repeatedly said no until we asked for the final time. Both Shannon and I asked together and said, "Please, can they stay? We promise we will be good and behave. We just want to catch more fireflies and have a contest."

I can remember by this time at night, they all had a couple of adult beverages and couldn't deny our request. Finally, they both said they could stay. All four of us were jumping up and down and went on to catch fireflies. We had a great night of fun until we finally passed out cold.

The next morning, we all slept in until my mother woke us up to tell us their grandmother was at the door.

"Are Billie Jo and David here with you?" she asked.

My mom and Dad said, "Yes they stayed the night with Shannon and Jessica."

"There was a fire at Billy's house last night. We were all frantic because we didn't know where the kids were. I finally found out from Hogman that the kids stayed with you!"

"My girls begged us last night for them to stay with us," said Mom. "And I am so thankful we did say yes because I would have never forgiven myself."

Bill's mother repeatedly told Mom thank you for letting them stay. "You saved them!" she kept saying.

I can remember hearing the conversation as I went downstairs first. Then the other kids came downstairs only to learn that Billie Jo and David's house had burnt to the ground. Billie Jo started crying, not knowing exactly what happened. Her grandmother told her that her dad would be ok. Their father and his friend Elmer wouldn't have made it out alive if it wasn't for the neighbor who helped get them out.

Naturally, we all were so incredibly thankful that they did. Most of all, my sister and I were thankful that we begged our parents to let Billie Jo and David spend the night because if we had not, who knows what would have happened. Being a kid, I was terrified at the thought that this could happen to any of us. One of my worst fears is a house fire. I believe that the fire at Billie Jo and David's house is why I have this deep-rooted fear of fire to this day. I am thankful today that my friends had angels to protect them.

***

The one person who has always stayed close to my heart was Barb. Barb was the one I looked up to all those years growing up, and I still do today. I don't ever have to worry about her being jealous of me or there being a lot of drama. We can talk about anything with each other and don't have to worry about talking behind the other's back. She is a true friend—loyal and honorable. I have gone to her on multiple occasions for advice, and she always provides clarity and common sense to all situations. I love her like a sister.

We have an endless amount of memories that we constantly laugh about when we get together. Like the time it was snowing heavy, lake effect snow, and we were craving Chinese food. Lake effect snow is a band of arctic air traveling over a warm body of water that produces heavy snow squalls. Even though we had several feet of snow, we still decided to go to Pulaski at the Dragon Garden to order food. Her husband, Steve, thought we were nuts, and we were as my car plowed snow with the front bumper.

When we arrived back at her house, I got out of the car knee-deep in snow. I looked around and didn't see her. I thought, *Wow, there's no way she's in the house already.* I walked in front of the car and called out her name. Suddenly, she jumped out towards me and threw a snowball at my face. It was more like an ice ball because when we got into the house, I had a black and blue ring starting to form along with red blood spots in my eyeball.

But even though that happened, we still laughed

and tackled each other, and we used her son Cody's sled to go sliding down the snowbanks and face plant in the snow. We always have a great time together, even when we were kids. We used to go swimming in my parent's pool and played Marco Polo. We would go fishing in our pond out back until the pond got leveled. We always joked around, even chasing each other with frogs or tadpoles. Well, I should say I did the chasing!

***

I remember having a man-made pond in our backyard that was there when my parents purchased the house. I was always up at the pond trying to catch tadpoles with a small net. My dad constantly stocked the pond with bass, perch, sunfish, and even bullhead that we caught from either Lake Ontario or the St. Lawrence River. It was always fun re-catching the fish and checking to see if they had multiplied.

I was always bummed if my worms died in the heat of the summer. I couldn't wait for it to rain because my father would say, "Dipper, let's go and pick some worms." It was messy, but I loved it! My sister and I would be outside at night picking up worms off the ground in the pouring rain because it was the only time we could get an abundance of worms for camp. My dad would always take care of the worms and feed them. Basically, we had our own little worm farm. We had a big styrofoam cooler that kept our worm farm fresh the whole time.

My dad always used to tell me to save worms for camp, but I would still sneak in the barn to take some up to the pond. He probably knew I was feeding the fish because as soon as I would put my line in the water, schools of fish would nibble on my hook so fast that the worm would be gone before I yanked my pole back. I thought it was fascinating to watch the fish go crazy over one worm. It's like the fish were starving or something.

My parents were eager to dispose of and level the pond completely. They knew it was starting to become too dangerous for my sister and me. My dad always went running for the 22 to shoot water moccasins that were coming from the pond. My mother was frightened that one day us kids were going to get bitten by these highly poisonous snakes. At that point, my parents discouraged us not to go up to the pond to fish anymore. I was sad, but then again, I didn't want to get bitten by those nasty snakes.

The final straw, the incident that finalized the pond being leveled, was me going downstairs to go outside one day. I reached for my wooden bat, and a water moccasin was curled up around the back hissing at me. I literally jumped out of my skin screaming. Right then and there, they made their decision—the pond was going to be leveled. So, they made arrangements with Steve Steinfeld to drain the pond and proceed to level the dirt, destroying it forever.

***

My mom loved horses. She just loved animals, but they got to be too much of an expense for the family. I remember running off the bus to see my mom's horse because she was pregnant. I actually witnessed a horse having a baby colt. It was an everyday thing to run to the barn, dropping my backpack on the way and jumping up the steps of the loft to overlook the horse's progress.

It was a great experience to have a horse growing up, but I don't ever remember riding the horse—only feeding her a handful of grass through the barb wire fence. I would pick the tall grass by the fence that wasn't able to be mowed and feed the horse and the colt all day long.

After the colt was old enough to run through the pasture, that's when my mother made the decision to sell her horses. I remember the devastation in my mother's eyes that she had to give up the one thing she loved the most. She kept all her saddles for the longest time, but she eventually sold them as well.

Years later, I found out the reason why she sold the horses. My father got laid off from Carrier Corporation and did not have the income to support the family and supply our needs. When I was young, I vaguely remember that my dad stayed with Uncle Wayne and Aunt Dolly for a while so he could go back to Canton University to further his education and get a better job.

I am thankful to my grandparents, John and Catherine Klock, for buying us school clothes and our necessities that my sister and I needed. I couldn't even imagine the sacrifices that my parents made to raise us. I always wondered where my brother was during my tender years; I do not remember.

My brother was not a memory for me. As I grew older, I learned more facts about him. My mother and father had to remove my brother from our house to protect my sister and me. My brother had bad habits; he would lie and steal. They told us that he was uncontrollable. As time progressed, I was able to meet my brother, but he was not able to stay with us. I never knew anything that happened when I was a baby concerning my brother. Do I choose not to know? Absolutely, because I don't want to know any more than I *want* to know. I just figured that if my brother wanted a sister-brother relationship, then he, being older, would pursue a relationship with me.

I begged for him and his family to come out and even made travel arrangements for my niece to bring him out, and he chose not to do so. I realized when I got married that there was no sense of trying anymore. I wanted to be a family and include my brother with everything we did. My mother and father invited him out for cookouts and family gatherings that he attended, but he didn't show for my wedding.

I thought for sure he wouldn't miss his youngest sister getting married. I wanted him in my life because, for many years, I didn't know him. I just wanted to know why he didn't come. I just felt it was excuse after excuse of him not having a ride, but when I talked to his daughter, she was going to bring him to the wedding with her. I guess it's just better off not knowing why anymore. Don't get me wrong, I love my brother, but I just wish our families were closer so we can understand his way of life.

***

After my father graduated from Canton College, he landed a great position at United Technologies as a dispatcher. He would dispatch technicians to fix chillers, yet another avenue to support our family. We were thankful to see our father every night after work, and it was refreshing that we were back on a schedule. My mother stopped working after she had me because they could not afford daycare back then. My mother would have had to work for free to keep me at the daycare, so they made the decision for her to stay home. She watched a couple of kids here and there to make extra money for Christmas.

I can recall for many years she made stuffed clowns and blankets to sell for money. She enjoyed doing it until her hands didn't work that much anymore. I loved everything she made for me, and I keep it close to my heart. She used to yell at me all the time to call her before I came home because she was making me a quilt. She would have to spread it out on the floor and pin it before sewing it. She made it obvious that it was being made for me because every time I would show up at the house, she would greet me at the door, saying, "You need to start calling me before you just pop in!"

"Ok, so what are you hiding from me?" I would smirk.

"None of your business!" Obviously, I saw it on the floor. By the time Christmas rolled around, I had completely forgotten about the quilt until I unwrapped it. I was so proud of that quilt because I know it was made with an abundance of love, and I knew my mother's hands were sore from the pricks from the needles. I knew that it was a lot of work to form and create a quilt, and that's why I cherish it with all my heart. I loved knowing that when I came home, my mother was always there. I actually envy her for having the privilege of being a housewife. It was nice to have a mother to stay home to cook and clean every day to support all of us.

In the same sense, I can also understand her frustrations being cooped up in the house with no interaction with the outside world until my father joined and became a member of the Jammers Biker Club. It was another fond memory of my childhood.

The Jammers Biker Club was like a second family to everyone. All the men and women were all so nice to all the children, and we were treated with love. Being part of the club kept my father very busy. I remember going to the club parties and listening to all the Harleys coming down the road. They were so loud that you could hear them from miles away. As a child, hearing the roar of the Harleys would get my adrenaline pumping. This always made me feel a part of them. I felt like a special child to be a part of the Harley family. It's an unforgettable feeling, and it will always remain that way.

My sister and I could only attend certain parties. One annual party was at Chris and Dresser Dick's house. Dresser Dick was a quiet tattoo artist who tattooed both my parents multiple times. His house was a regular kid-friendly place with a pool and volleyball net set up in the back. We used to ride bikes and even go check on the chickens to see if they laid any eggs to bring up to the house.

For the most part, if you asked for something, anyone would be more than willing to help you. Everyone would bring their kids too, so we all played together. My sister and I would play with his daughter all the time. She was younger than us and was Chris and Dresser's only child.

The parties there were fun and exciting. They would start on a Friday and continue to Sunday. Tents were pitched, so nobody was driving drunk. As you can imagine, nobody was ever sober at these parties besides the children and even then, who knows; teenagers were teenagers. After Dresser Dick passed away, there were no more parties there. It was a devastating time for the Jammers to lose one of their members. It took a while for the club to mentally regroup after the loss of Dresser Dick.

The clubhouse was a hangout for all the Jammers. I can remember the clubhouse was located not that far from Mary Karen's lake house in Bridgeport, New York. They would host parties there for the members and continue to have club meetings and holiday parties there as well. All the members were great people. Some were more friendly toward kids than others. My parents developed a close relationship with many of the Jammers, and I will always consider them to be my second mom and dad.

***

You could always tell who loved you by how they stepped in and took care of you. Aunt Deb and Uncle Rich were one couple that I looked up to as a child, and I still do to this day. They were not part of the club but were always at club functions. They had three boys—Dave, Wayne, and Keith—who grew up with my sister and me. We still keep in touch and attend some of their family functions. Aunt Deb and Uncle Rich are always there for me, regardless of what is happening in my life. They are always there supporting our family. To me, they *are* family. Lee and Byrd are husband and wife, and Byrd was involved with the Jammers just as much as John was with his wife, Audrey. They all were really close to my parents as well.

As I got older, I realized that they were my Harley family for life, and they would always be there for me no matter what. I love them very much! They were together on their bikes the majority of the time traveling to different events. My mom didn't ride as much; however, she would travel wherever Dad and the Jammers went. Mom used to drive a brown Ford Econoline Cargo Van, which had a love seat in the back for my sister and me to sit on. If one of the bikes broke down, then they would load the Harley up in Mom's van. My dad always carried his tool set in the van for minor fixes when we traveled.

My mom was a brute in her younger years. She used to tell us stories about how she would protect the women in the club, especially Aunt Deb, Aunt Laurie, Mary Karen, Lee, Donna, and Audrey. They used to hang out at Jump in Jacks in Syracuse—a popular bar for motorcycle clans back then. The Hell's Angels used to hang out there too. A run-in with a rival club would always end up in a fight when they would flash their colors.

I can recall my mother telling me a story about how a Hell's Angels' wife cornered my mom's friend Lee in the bathroom. My mom went looking for her and found Leigh in the bathroom being threatened. So, my mother took the wife, threw her in the stall, pushed her head into the toilet, and flushed her hair. Needless to say, my mother developed quite a reputation-stay away from the Jammer's old ladies.

So, no matter where the club was at, the club's wives always stayed close to my mother. My mother doesn't deal with drama very well. She will be the first one to speak her mind and tell the truth. I realized later in life that I inherited that quality from her.

Most of the Jammers got along with the majority of the motorcycle clubs. The Night Stalkers always associated with the Jammers and were included with most of the Jammers events, especially Chris and Dresser Dick's annual house parties. The Night Stalker Club was a family-oriented organization as well. Very friendly and always lending a hand if needed.

I used to french braid all the club member's wives' hair. Of course, it's easier to put a helmet on when your hair is braided. I know that for a fact because I had long hair to my butt growing up, and I would braid my hair when I used to ride with my Dad. I loved riding with my father; it was less dangerous than it is now. All the ladies would tip me for doing their hair. They always pointed me out, and if I wasn't around, the women would complement my mother of what a talented girl I was. I have been french braiding since I was 6 years old. At the age of 8, I decided that I wanted to grow up to be a cosmetologist.

***

During the summer months, we would attend some club functions. We were not allowed to all of them because the adults would get rowdy and drunk. On the rare occasion that we could not attend a Jammer party, we would stay home with the babysitter, which was always a bummer. It caused more drama than anything. Mom hated to leave us with a sitter, but at some point, she needed to get out and associate with people and have a normal conversation. She needed a change from looking at four walls every day of every week.

It was a tough life for my mother too. If she was unable to bring us to an adult party, then she couldn't go unless she found a sitter. When you get initiated into the club, you have to perform special duties. The club had a President, Vice President, Secretary, Treasurer, Striker, etc. Each member is designated to perform a specific duty or order from the President. My dad had to perform duties that were asked from the club members to carry out different things like attend all meetings, taking care of the club house, organizing club parties, and many more activities.

There were many things that he did for the club that I wouldn't even know because I was little. But in the same sense, they would have parties that children were not allowed to attend. The club did have family parties for Easter, Christmas, July 4th, Thanksgiving, and back to school. They always did things for us kids as a family.

But when Dad had to be with the club for a certain club function that was mandatory, my dad had to go, no questions asked. I could always remember my dad leaving on the Harley, and my mom would have to meet him there. The Jammers were continuously putting a damper on my family's life sometimes because we could never go on vacation or to the beach. Once initiated, your obligation was to the club.

***

My parents met a lot of different club members during their years with the Jammers. The Kingsman Club is one that they met at the Change of Seasons

Party at Panther Lake. The Kingsman party at our house was crazy. Percy, the President of the Kingsman and his wife Duck, were amazing people. Their club was based out of Buffalo, New York. They traveled for hours to get to my parents' house.

I could hear the Kingsman Club riding their Harleys on I-81 even before they exited off the interstate. Miles and miles of just Harleys roaring down the road was a sight to see. Feeling the ground beneath your feet rumbling was exciting to me as a child. I thought that I was so cool being a part of a nomad motorcycle club.

All of the Kingsman and Night Stalkers stayed at the house that evening after the night's festivities. My sister and I woke up to people sleeping everywhere and anywhere they could lay their heads. We even found people sleeping in our bathtub. My sister and I decided to brew pots and pots of hot coffee and sold it to everyone the morning after for a quarter.

Man, we made out like bandits. We told everyone that we were saving up for school clothes which we were at that time because we were not a wealthy family. We even collected all the beer cans over the weekend. After recycling the cans and returning the bottles, we ended up with $375.00 to go school shopping. I don't ever remember saying thank you to everyone for that donation, so I want to thank everyone now.

Most of the guys and their wives were scary looking but really nice. I think the men appeared mean because they sported tattoos up their arms and wore their hair pulled back in a ponytail braided to the end. All the men had their club patches on a jean jacket vest to mark which club they belonged to.

While most were good people, you always knew which men to stay away from. Most importantly, they all were kind to us children because if not, my mother and father would have to protect us from them. Or I should say my mother would kick their asses.

There were many people who were afraid of my mother back in those days because she was not scared of saying how she felt or mention to others that they were wrong. Due to the fact that she was straight forward, she had a reputation that spoke volumes about her character. She protected her friends but, more importantly, our family.

***

Lee, Audrey, Aunt Deb, Mary Karen, Donna, and Aunt Laurie were very close to my mother. They meant the world to me as a child as well. These women are amazing mothers with huge hearts who cared for my sister and me at all times. Aunt Deb and Aunt Laurie are not blood relations at all, but I consider them as my second mothers as I do with them all.

Aunt Deb has watched me grow to the woman I am today. I love and adore that she was always there for me. Aunt Laurie, God bless her soul, battled diabetes for many years and was taken from us too early in life. I love her so much. She always used to call me her Gondue. Apparently, I always filled my diaper when I was a baby. She was a sensitive and loving Native American woman that I miss so much each and every day. It saddens me that she missed so much of my life, but I always knew she was watching over my family and me.

I will always remember going to Mary Karen's house for many of the Jammers parties on Oneida Lake. It was located on a road without much traffic, so all of us kids could go for a walk and play in the street. Back then, things seemed to be simpler. Many of my memories involve my Jammer friends growing up. Byrd and Lee's children are Jennifer, Crystal, and Lisa. Jennifer and Crystal were closer in age to my sister Shannon then they were to me, but Lisa and I were close in age. Uncle Rich and Aunt Deb had three boys—Dave, Wayne, and Keith—who I always considered brothers to me. Mary Karen only had one child, Tara, who is younger than my sister and I, but we spent many days at their house growing up. John and Audrey had little John and Jamie. We all were always together, and we all are still close to this day in spirit.

I can remember going for a walk with Crystal and Jennifer while they were sneaking wine coolers from the party. They were 18 and 20 at the time, so it really didn't seem like a big deal. I always laughed my butt off when I was around those two. They both have great personalities, and I would laugh so hard my abs would hurt.

After my dad left the club, our lives were all about family and everyday living. I was getting older and becoming more aware of events happening around me. I began participating in school activities, including sports, year-round.

***

My school years at Altmar Elementary were very memorable. I loved being in grade school, and our Christmas concert was such a big event for our school. Mr. Lopez, our music teacher, was awesome.

Our school prepared for this concert for months, and it felt so special every year. We used to have Christmas parties with milk and cookies, and our teacher would give us candy bags to bring home. Even better, we would make Christmas gifts for Mom and Dad.

I loved the fact that my mother was dedicated to bringing me to dance classes every Tuesday and Thursday at the Parish Elementary School. Miss Ellen was my dance instructor. Her mother sat at a desk to collect the dance and costume fees. Her mother was so nice and always had a smile on her face. Miss Ellen was very nice as well. She was absolutely beautiful and an amazing dancer. I thought that when I grew up, I wanted to be just as talented as her. I can remember the day I was picked to be the first solo dancer and receive an award for being an outstanding dancer.

"Ladies," Miss Ellen said to the class. "I am so proud of each and every one of you. This year, I am going to pick out one dancer whom I feel deserves a solo dance in the final recital finale. Each year I will continue to reward you with recognition of your efforts. This year we choose Jessica Rainess to be our first solo dancer of the year."

I looked at her completely surprised! I couldn't

believe it. I was about to cry, so she came up to me, giving me a hug at the end of class and saying, "I am so proud of you, and I am excited to see you perform your first solo."

"Miss Ellen, thank you so much for everything," I said with a grin. "I want to be just like you when I grow up. Thank you for believing in me."

"There is nothing to believe in besides what is in your heart, honey," said Mrs. Ellen. "I know you will be fantastic. We have a lot of work to do, so go and tell your mom the good news and I will see you next week!"

I felt so special, and I couldn't let her down. I remember practicing every day on my solo routine. When it was time to order my dance costume, Miss Ellen pulled me aside after class, sat me down next to her mother, and showed me what she wanted me to wear for the solo. I was so amazed at how spectacular the costume she had picked for me was. It was a beautiful light pink leotard with a sheer flowy skirt. I remember being so excited. More importantly, she made me feel super special the day of our recital.

After dancing to my jazz, tap, and hip-hop routines, it was finally hitting me that I was going to do my first solo dance. I was starting to get butterflies before I started my solo. My body started getting warm, and I was scared that I was going to faint in front of everyone.

Miss Ellen saw the look on my face. "Honey, are you ok? You don't look ok," she asked, concerned.

"I am getting warm and fuzzy like I am going to pass out on stage," I admitted.

"It's normal to have butterflies, but go sit down over here and just breathe. You will be perfect. Plus, you have me to look at if you need me."

"How long before I hit the stage?"

"You have about 4 acts in front of you, so I would say about 20 minutes. So just breathe! You got this!"

I nodded and went to sit down for a little bit to regroup. I can remember that I froze and went blank, but she saved me. When she saw me panicking, she started to dance with me behind the curtain. Once I saw her, I instantly got back on track. I was relieved that I didn't mess up that bad, and she gave me a hug and said I did fantastic.

After the recital was over, she was recognizing the parents along with the students and thanking all of them for their support and love for the program. I was shocked when she called me to the stage, gave me flowers with an award for being such a great student, and expressed how proud she was of me. I felt a little embarrassed but proud that she gave me that opportunity to shine.

As I progressed from grade school to middle school, I knew that the change would be a difficult task. As time drew closer for me to begin middle school, I was scared. When I got into sports in 6th-8th grade, I felt more and more confident. I usually kept to myself a lot during those years; I didn't want to be known. I didn't feel like I could bring a lot to the table. Remember, I came from a poor family that did what we had to do to survive.

Back then, we were too quick to judge others for what they were wearing or how they acted. Nowadays, it's even worse than it was back then. I was neutral in most cases; however, I would never let anyone pick on others that were less fortunate because I knew how that felt. For example, my mom would only take us up to Ames department store or shop through JCPenney's catalog. We never went to the mall to check out different stores. Some kids would come to school with holes in their shoes and ragged clothing, and I felt bad for them and stuck up for them when they got teased.

I realized that my parents lived within their means of what they could afford. It wasn't that they didn't *want* to take us to the mall, it was because they couldn't afford what we might have wanted in the mall and didn't want to see us disappointed. I understand that my parents did a great job with what they had to work with for Shannon and me. Because at the end of the day, it could have been much worse than it was. At that point, I didn't complain, I was just thankful.

Once I began playing sports, I learned that people could learn to love you for you. I love to make people laugh, and that was my gift. If I could act goofy and make someone laugh, I considered that my good deed for that day. I was far from being popular, but I did hang out with some popular girls in school. I talked to a little of everyone. Most of the popular kids I interacted with played sports as well.

I played sports year-round: soccer, basketball, track & field, and softball. I think sports was my motivation for attending school each and every day. Sports motivated me to keep up my grades. If I allowed my grades to slip, I would have been riding the bench watching everyone else play. This would have been devastating to me, so I kept my head in the books.

I can remember that my parents would never miss a home game. They loved watching me play sports, and to this day, they still come to my softball games. Even though I enjoyed playing sports and was good at it, I felt I wanted to do something more.

One day, I decided to go to the guidance office and apply for my working papers. I started to work at the age of 14 at the Liberty Bell Restaurant in Parish. It was a great family restaurant, and it was classy. It was one of those places that you would get all dressed up to go and eat a three-course meal.

My first position was washing dishes back in the kitchen. Washing dishes wasn't that easy, especially after dinner hours. There were a lot of pots and pans, but I knew that if I started working, I could save money for a car and buy the clothes that I wanted to buy. I was still able to play sports year-round, go to school, and do my homework every day when I had my job. My boss would always work around my schedule, which was awesome. She was the best boss I ever had. She was so nice and thoughtful.

I can remember getting my first bonus from her, one hundred dollars. I thought that she overpaid me at first, and I remember asking her about it after my shift.

"I noticed in my paycheck that I was overpaid by $100," I said slowly. "And I wanted you to know so you can fix it before I leave?"

"No honey," she chuckled, "I didn't overpay you. It is your Christmas bonus, and you deserve it."

I looked at her with confusion and started to smile. "Thank you so much! I didn't expect it at all," I said happily.

"You all work hard all year long, this is my Christmas gift to you."

I gave her a hug. "Thank you, it means a lot to me."

"I know, honey, now don't keep your parents waiting any longer. I will see you tomorrow."

I didn't know how to react but be grateful and say thank you. After a year of working with her, she promoted me to a hostess—greeting and seating our guests. I loved my job even more because the waitresses would tip me for helping them clean their tables so other guests can sit down quickly. I don't have a bad memory of that place.

I was very thankful to my mother and father for providing all of my transportation needs. I know it had to be frustrating for them to come pick me up at 11 p.m. when it was snowing and the wind was blowing outside. I can remember the weekends when it was nice outside, but they couldn't make plans because they had to drop me off and pick me up. I remember how hot it got in the kitchen during the summer months working every weekend. I did feel at some point that I was missing out on summer activities with my friends and family. I especially missed the entertainment at the Happy Valley parties with my best friends.

The Happy Valley parties during my late teenage years were always amusing. Happy Valley is miles and miles of state land with awesome fishing holes, hunting spots, and snowmobile trails. Of course, there were keg parties too. We would always hear stories about the KKK haunting the Happy Valley area.

We were always scared to drive by this one white abandoned house. My childhood best friends were Scott and Gary. They would always pick me up, and we always had the greatest times together. I can remember Gary telling me one day on our way to fish that the people that lived there would chase us down the road if we stopped in front of their house. Scott would make up stuff as they would go along just to scare the pants off me. Not sure how much of these tales are true, but they have definitely been spoken of several times.

I can remember Scott, Gary, and some of our close friends going ghost hunting. I never really believed in the stories until I actually experienced it firsthand. I can remember Scott and Gary hearing a story about the Lady in White. So apparently, the story is about a woman who was wedded to a man by a prearranged marriage. She didn't want to be married to this man, so on her wedding day, she decided to end her life by jumping off the train as it crossed a bridge over water. Thus, the Lady in White was born.

Now, these railroad tracks were abandoned, and nobody walked them because of the history behind this story. Some people said they saw the Lady in White haunting the bridge at night. So, Scott and Gary came up with the idea of us going so we can walk the trail and the train rails. We went a couple of times and experienced different things until one night, we all were running back to our vehicles.

I can remember Scott, Penny, Gary, Brian, Ben, Mike, Mariah, Lonny, and Michelle ended up going. We all were walking down with flashlights to the bridge where the Lady in White supposedly jumped. Gary was literally walking back from the middle of the bridge when all of a sudden, a white ball of light appeared and started getting bigger and bigger.

"Gary, look behind you!" we screamed.

"Oh, shit!" he yelled and started running toward all of us as we are running down the trail back to our vehicles. Whatever it was, it was following us until we got to the parking lot, and it disappeared.

Back then Scott, Ben, Lonny, and Mike had CB radios in which you can talk back and forth to each other on different radio frequencies. I can remember vaguely that the guys were saying how freaky it was to see the white light and that it was following us.

Gary dropped his flashlight in the trail, and Lonny asked, "Are you going to go get it?"

"Fuck no!" shouted Gary. "Are you nuts? You go get it!"

We all started laughing. Suddenly, we all heard a woman screaming through the CB Radios. We all were blaming each other for making the screams, so we all got out of our vehicles to talk. Then, we heard a woman screaming *again*.

We all looked at each other and said, "Screw this, I am out of here!"

"Hurry up!"

We all were about to shit our pants. I was dating Ben at the time, so he dropped me off at home. I got in the house and locked the door. I slept in my parents' room downstairs, and I was lying in bed scared out of my mind because I was constantly hearing glass breaking inside the house. I literally thought someone had broken in.

I called Ben, freaking out. "Ben, you need to come over right now. I keep hearing glass breaking, and I think someone is in the house. You need to come over."

"Ok, I am on my way."

He shows up at my house with a baseball bat and calls me. "Come unlock the door!" he shouted.

"Ok," I said shakily as I am getting the nerve to bolt through the house. As soon as I unlock the door, he says, "Stay far behind me just in case I start swinging."

He checks every room in the house and goes to check upstairs. As he is coming down, he says to me, "There is nobody here, you nerd!"

"I swear I heard glass breaking in my house loud and clear!"

"Well, there is nobody in the house."

I just about begged him to stay because I was so scared. So, we both fell asleep on the couch until morning and then he went home. When my mom came home, I told her about what had happened.

"You have to be careful because sometimes ghosts can attach themselves to you and come home with you," she said seriously.

I looked at her with my eye about to pop out of my sockets. "Are you serious?" I asked.

"Yes, I am serious! I wouldn't be doing that anymore!"

I told Scott and Gary what my mother said, and they looked at me like I was nuts and ready to check into a looney bin for the weekend. I don't think I ever went ghost hunting again.

Scott, Gary, and I were called the Three Musketeers because we were always together. Never would you see one without the other. I still remember one Happy Valley party that we went to, a car caught on fire. Supposedly a car was leaking gas, and some kid decided to light a lighter to see where the leak was in the dark. Apparently, he had no common sense. The car engulfed into flames, and everyone thought the car was going to explode. We could hear the sirens, and everyone began scattering, grabbing the kegs, and taking off.

We left, and Scott dropped me off first and then Gary. Just as I was getting into bed, Scott called my house at 1 a.m.

"Hey, I need your help. My tire fell off, and I need a jack," he explained.

"Don't you have a jack in the truck?"

"No, because the jack I need won't lift the truck to get the tire on because of the lift."

"Ok, I will be right there, Shithead."

"Ok, Dipper."

When I came, Scott's tire fell off his truck and was rolling down the road. Scott, forever the jokester, said, "I was just driving down the road, and all of a sudden I seen my tire flying by me. I thought I was just hallucinating at first until sparks started flying."

"You're lucky that you didn't get into an accident."

"This is not the first time this happened."

"What do you mean not the first time?"

"When I went to have the tires put on, they put the wrong lug nuts on the truck. So, I am waiting for the right ones to come in."

"Well, it looks like I will be driving from now on!"

"Nope, Dipper, I don't go anywhere without my truck."

"Well, you better be getting new lug nuts for your baby before I get in it again."

My mom was frantic and worried that something may have happened to Scott, so I had to go get Scott and Gary. I reassured her that everything was fine and to go back to sleep. My parents' minds were at ease when they knew I was with Scott and Gary. We always had fun, there was never a dull moment, and my folks always knew I was safe with them.

***

I will never forget my best friends, Barb and Steve's bachelor and bachelorette party. The girls went their separate ways from the men. We ended up at Sam's Lakeside dancing and having a great time; that's when it *was* a nice place to hang out. We all got back to Barb's house before the men did, so what did I do? Well, let's just say I took someone's truck through the Valley mud pits at 2 a.m.

I knew where all Scott's hiding spots for his keys were. I always told him someday someone might steal his truck. Little did he know it would be me, hahaha. So, I looked behind his front tire, not there. Looked in the flap to the gas tank, bingo! I knew Scott wouldn't be mad at me because he never gets mad.

So, we all piled in the cab and the back bed and took a nice muddy stroll through the valley. We made it back to Barb's house just before the men arrived. Scott gets out of Steve's vehicle and takes a look at his truck and says, "Wow, my truck is dirty," while all of us are laughing because he is blaming Gary for taking it.

"Every time you take my truck, you always bring it back dirty," said Scott.

"Scott, I didn't take your truck, I was with you all night," said Gary calmly.

"Well, I don't know how it got dirty then because I just washed it."

"How could I have possibly taken your truck, Bub, if I was with you all night?"

"Well, if you weren't off sniffing all those girls all night, who knows where you were?"

"You wish you had girls to sniff!"

"Gary, why does it always have to come down to who sniffs who?"

"Why don't you go stiff your seat like a hound dog and figure out who took your truck!"

"I don't want to smell your ass!"

At this point, the rest of us are all about to pee our pants. Those two bickered for a little while. They sounded like an old married couple trying to figure it out. The fact that they were drunk made it all the more hilarious. None of us women decided to tell Scott that it was me that took his truck through the valley that night, that is, at least not until a few years later. To this day, we all laugh about the exchange between those two from that night.

Scott and Gary would fight off and on like crazy, but the next day, they would kiss and make up like it never happened. No, I don't mean that literally. They are both straight and love girls very much. As you can imagine, I didn't always fit into their bromance because I was a girl. When they used to ask a girl out, I would scare the girl away. They would always feel threatened by my friendship with the guys. It worked both ways also. Guys were scared to ask me out as well.

When I started dating, we drifted a little bit. Scott and Gary told me to break up with my boyfriend at the time because they missed me. I can remember we made a pact that if we were single until the age of 30, I would marry Scott, and if I was single still and Scott was married, then I would marry Gary. However, we did not honor that pact. I had bigger dreams for my future than to be settled down, so I decided to go to college and continue to spend time with my buddies in my spare time.

After I graduated high school, I really wanted to go into the Marines. While I wanted to join the Marines, my father was not in favor of that idea at all. He encouraged me to give college a try for a year. We agreed that if I didn't like it, then I could enlist and join the Marines.

I decided to go to Jefferson Community College and get an Associate's Degree as a Paralegal. I got accepted into the program and was on top of my game in school. I developed new relationships with friends and went to parties every weekend like a normal college student would. I loved my life. I worked nights and weekends at Fat Nancy's Tackle Shop while I pursued my education. What could possibly go wrong? I was responsible, paying my own bills, and I had goals to achieve.

I grew close to and became friends with a group of students from a town called Mexico located in New York. I met a funny guy named Jason. He was known as Howie, and we became really great friends. Many people told us we acted exactly alike. I can remember one instance in which Howie took the spare tire out of the back of his wheel well and filled it with beer and ice. It was our luck to get a flat tire at midnight, but like he said, "At least we have the beer."

He was a comical guy, but he would always keep a straight face. He sure knew how to put a smile on my face. He used to say that he loved to see me smile all the time. We were so close that Howie and I used to switch vehicles. I would drive his Dodge Stratus to college, and he put a stereo system in my Chevy Cavalier with subs and tinted my windows for me. He always had an idea on how to deck out my car. We were constantly on an adventure.

I can remember a Halloween night when our little group of friends were all roaming the roads in the Town of Mexico, New York. We all decided to crash at Howie's house. I will never forget how quiet his mother was and how boisterous his father was about all of us staying in their basement. There were a bunch of us that's for sure.

I can remember his dad calling him upstairs to yell at him, but Howie was so calm. He would just make smart comments and walk away. He was so spoiled. I am sure if all of our friends remembered that night, they would be giggling right now because it was one for the books.

Unfortunately, all our nights were not this sweet. There was a night that was horrible. It was worse than we could ever imagine. One night I will never forget is when a few of us went to Oswego to hang out at a bar, playing darts and shooting pool. We all left at around the same time, but this time, Howie wasn't driving my car—he drove his friend's car that was the same make and model as mine but a different year. I never expected anything to ever happen to him because he was always a safe driver. I would trust him to drive everywhere we went but that night he got into a car accident.

I will never forget the day I received the phone call from Tommy the next morning. I just woke up, and I was in the kitchen with my mom. Tommy was calling, so I answered.

"Hey, buddy, what's up. What are you doing?" I asked.

"Hey, I need to tell you something. You need to sit down. I have some really bad news," he said in a sad voice.

"What is it?"

"Howie is in the hospital in critical condition. He may not make it. Apparently, he was driving another car like yours and missed a curve and went off the road and hit a bulldozer. I don't know the whole story."

Instantly, I dropped to my knees and began to cry.

"Bobbo and I just came from the hospital," he continued. "We don't want you to go and see him. We want you to remember him the way he was."

I couldn't say anything but just cry into the phone.

"I am coming over right now, you can't be by yourself right now."

"Ok," I cracked through my hysterical cries. I stood up from the floor, and my mom knew that something bad had happened. She hugged me as I cried in her arms.

"Baby, I am so sorry. God has his way. He had better plans for Howie, and it wasn't here on earth."

"Why, Mom? Why!" I cried.

"Honey, I wish I had an answer for you. I really do because if we all knew the answer, it would make us come to terms with things, but we don't have those answers."

At this point, I can hear Tommy coming down the road in his grey low rider truck, blaring the music that we all listened to all the time. Tommy came with Bobbo to my house to pick me up to go be with our friends. The look in their eyes was devastating. They ended up staying with me for a while to keep an eye on me, but in the back of my head, I wanted to go up to the hospital. They insisted that I stayed with them. I think that they already knew that he was gone but was waiting for confirmation. Finally, we got the call saying he was gone.

A piece of my heart died that day. I was on an emotional roller coaster and couldn't control my crying. My parents talked to me over and over again to console me. They promised that it would get easier, but it did not seem that way at the time. I played that night over and over in my head. I blamed myself for not looking after him and telling him that he could have driven my car that night because my car drove differently and was modified into a sportier car than the one he drove that night. I think he expected it to ride the same as my car, which it did not.

I had low profiles on my car, and he had standard tires on the car he drove. The low-profile tire is a smaller tire with rims that made my car turn corners faster and was lower to the road, giving my car a better advantage with corners. My car hugged the road tight around curves, and the car he was driving did not. I was so sorry for being the first one to leave that night and not being there to speak up to tell Howie that he was going home with me and to try and change that night's outcome.

It took over a year for me to understand and accept that he was never coming back and would never pull into my driveway again. I was lost. I quit college and told my parents I needed a semester off. I was going to parties with our friends, thinking I would see him and wishing I could get some closure.

Then one day, I met Joe. He knew me, and I knew of him, but I didn't know Joe on a personal level before then. All I knew was that Joe and I went to the same school together but never hung out. He knew that Howie and I were very close. As time progressed, Joe and I began hanging out a lot. We both had a lot of mutual friends; Howie was one of them. Joe's cousins Kirk and Joelon went to school with Howie, so it was a continuous circle of friends.

One evening when we were in Williamstown, Joe decided to have a bonfire. He promised Howie that night that he would take care of me. Joe knew that I was having a hard time accepting the fact that Howie was gone and that he was never coming back. At that moment, I felt secure knowing that I had someone to lean on through that hard time. I didn't date anyone for the longest time by choice, but I decided to date Joe in time. As time went on, I was getting more and more attracted to him because he always made me laugh because of his goofiness.

After three months of him trying to get close to me, I finally broke down and showed that I cared about him. Losing Howie made me realize that nothing is promised. I loved him so much, and it all was taken away in an instant. Joe and I made a great couple, and we never fought. We lived each day of our lives together to the fullest. I truly adored Joe and his personality.

Joe and I dated for years and shared many memories together. As a result, I got really close with Joe's sister, Jessica. We would drink coffee and talk all the time. She was both bold and honest with you know matter what. I was working for Carrier Corporation off and on since I was 18, but then after a year, I got laid off again. Jessica helped me get a job working with her at Cedar Pines as a waitress and bartender. We had good times at Cedar Pines, and the restaurant had a group of girls that everyone would come and see. Gena, Valerie, Crystal, Heather, Jessica, and Darlene (Jessica and Joe's mom) worked with us. We all were awesome bartenders and servers.

Joe would drop me off and pick me up after work. One night, Jessica was driving home with Dave Durgan, and she didn't make the curve. Suddenly, she ran right into a snowbank. She was lucky she didn't hit the tree beyond it. I can remember seeing them in front of us because we were following when the car suddenly stopped. The snow was thick that night, so it was a little hard to see. Joe and I stopped on the side of the road, and Dave gets out of the car.

"Joe," said Dave. "You need to drive your sister's car. She just hit a snowbank. I kept telling her to turn! Turn! Turn!! And she just kept going straight! She kept telling me that it wasn't time to turn, apparently!"

Jessica got out of the car and said with a giggle, "Don't listen to him; he doesn't know what he is talking about."

"Apparently, I don't" said Dave, "because there is your car, and that is definitely a snowbank!"

Joe and I never laughed so hard in our lives because of the way Dave explained how it happened. He was a total character. Jessica had a contagious laugh that made all of us die laughing with her. We just loved it when she started drinking and laughing. We all would get to laughing because we love her so much. All of us in Williamstown—Paige, Todd, Jason, Dave and some others—would get together all the time and hang out. We all had a blast no matter what we did because Joe was always the center of attention with all his joking.

Joe and I got along great, and we never used to fight until the end. We were engaged to be married for a year until we decided to split. Our relationship wasn't perfect, but we loved each other. I never thought I would love anyone as much as I loved him, and I was hoping someday I would be wrong.

One thing about Joe was that he was a jealous man. He didn't like anyone looking or even talking to me. He always said it wasn't me that he didn't trust, it was everyone else. I think that jealousy was what broke us up. I wanted to have more adventures in life, and he was scared to let me spread my wings.

Deep down inside, I believe that we both knew that we would always love each other no matter what happened between us, but we separated and went our own ways. I was okay at first, but after weeks went by, I felt empty and wanted him back. It wasn't long after that my life began to spiral out of control after we split. For the past 5 years, all I knew how to do was to be with and spend time with Joe.

***

I continued to work every day. I got my job back at Carrier Cooperation and was making great money. As luck would have it, I got laid off again, and that is when my life hit rock bottom: partying all the time, hanging out with the wrong crowd, and making bad choices. I learned quickly how life could change in an instant.

I got into my first car accident on Christmas Eve and was in the hospital for the holidays. When I was hit head on while I was at a dead stop, I had never felt such an impact. I can remember being hit so hard that my seat was pushed almost completely into the passenger's seat above the dash. I blacked out because my head went through the windshield. I was starting to come to when I realized blood gushing from my face and nose. I felt myself choking as a result of the blood slowly filling up my lungs. I really thought I was going to die that day.

I remember a man with black hair opening my door to my truck. "Stay with me," he said calmly. "The ambulance and help is on its way." He came closer to me and cupped his hands around my chin to stop me from choking on my own blood.

"Keep breathing," he kept repeating. "You're okay."

I was listening, but it was getting more and more difficult to stay awake. I felt myself drifting into a sleep when suddenly I heard the sound of the ambulance pulling up to the scene and the EMT trying to get me out the truck.

The next thing I remember was when I heard my mother screaming for me as I was in the ambulance. Trooper Parker walked her over to see me, and all I saw were the tears pouring down her cheeks.

"Me and your dad are on our way to the hospital right now," she promised.

I was in so much pain, and no medicine they gave me relieved my suffering.

I remember the look in my dad's eyes, seeing how worried he was about me because I was pretty banged up. Next thing I remember is going in for emergency surgery.

It was right then and there that I knew I had an angel and realized my life had to change for the better. The wreck was so bad that I can remember having multiple surgeries on my nose, elbow, and even my head. No, I didn't have any brain damage, but I had a lot of glass in my head.

Joe's father, Chuck, drove all the way from Rochester to sit with me so that I would not be alone on Christmas. The weather was bad, and my parents didn't want to stay at the hospital and fight the weather in the dark. That's why they didn't stay at the hospital with me. I will never be able to thank Chuck for taking their places for that night. When I really need someone, he was there.

Once I came home, I sat there and cried to my mom that I never wanted to be alone again. After that, I knew my life was about to change, and I was going to be the person I wanted to be. I was told that after my accident I was unable to have children. Finding this bit of news out completely devastated me. The thing for which a woman's body was uniquely designed, I could no longer do. Little did I know what was going to happen in the future!

Time had went by and I happened to run into the EMT members from my car accident. They asked me how I was and commented on how much better I looked from the last time they saw me.

"Yes," I responded. "I am doing much better, but still going through surgeries. But I wanted to ask you if you remember the gentleman with the black hair who helped me in my truck ? I really would like to thank him."

The guys looked at each other in confusion.

"Jess," said one of them. "There was no one in your truck. We had to use the jaws of life to get into your truck in order to get you out. I wish I had an answer, but it sounds like you had a guardian angel watching over you."

I was stunned. "Are you sure?" I asked. "Because he kept telling me to breathe."

"No," he said confused. "It's impossible."

I was speechless. I knew what I saw. I couldn't believe that all this had happened, and no one even saw him. I still remember everything about his features. His hair, his outfit, the sound of his voice, and even his hands touching my flesh to keep me stable. I truly believe that I had an angel looking out for me that day. This great unsolved mystery still resonates deep within my spirit, and I truly hope to discover the answer someday.

So, here I was going through all the repercussions of that car accident. I dealt with all the surgeries, MRIs, x-rays, and medications. I was continuously having nerve blocks from Dr. Tiso and trigger point injections from Dr. Profetto. I was thankful to have such amazing doctors to help me recover. Truth be told, I was in bad shape. I still see my favorite doctor, Dr. Profetto, from time to time for my pain. He took care of me for many years after my accident. I know to this day I am his favorite patient because I bring him coffee the way he likes it.

I never had my menstrual cycle since before my accident. In the back of my head, I was wishing that someday, I would be gifted a miracle and have a child. The summer of 2003, I met a younger man who seemed mature for his age named Philip. We went to the Monster Truck Jam together and hung out a couple of times. The more time I spent with him, the surer I was that we were not going to be a good fit for each other. I tried to end it before it went on any further, but he kept showing up to my house unannounced without permission. I thought it was a red flag, annoying.

We only hung out for a couple months before I realized that I wasn't feeling like myself. Before I knew it, I was gaining weight, couldn't stand the smell of cigarette smoke, and I even quit smoking them myself.

One day, I asked him, "Would you like to go to my cousin's wedding with me? I wanted to tell you that I have been feeling really sick, and I think I should take a pregnancy test to make sure that I'm not pregnant."

"Ya, I can go with you. We can stop and get tests on the way back."

"That was my plan."

"Ok!"

He knew that I was in a bad car accident, and I was still trying to recover. I did have to remind him of what my doctor had told me about my uterus and that I wouldn't be able to get pregnant. Remember how I mentioned that I was on a lot of medication? Well, one of them was Topamax. Fun fact: You're not supposed to conceive a child while taking this medication. Just my luck, right?

After the wedding, we purchased several pregnancy tests and went back to my house. My parents were still at the wedding, but I knew we were going to expect them back soon. As I took the first test, it came out positive, and I kind of shrugged it off. *No, this is impossible*, I thought to myself. Then I took the second one and then the third one, finally coming to the realization that this must be true. I *am* pregnant.

I was completely in shock. A slew of thoughts came to mind. I was nervous and scared that I wouldn't be able to carry my baby to term. On top of that, I knew that the relationship I was in was not a healthy one.

I had horrible thoughts of miscarrying and the baby being unhealthy. I thought about if all the surgeries I'd undergone could harm the fetus. With all these thoughts permeating my mind, I decided to shut them out completely. I was not going to give up because if this was going to be my only chance to give birth to a child, then I was going to take my chance. I told myself that God would only give me what I could handle.

Despite all my doubts and fears, I decided to keep the baby. I gave Philip a choice. He could either stand by my side and try to work on things, or he could walk away, and I would not ask for anything from him. He chose to stick by me. For whatever reason, after we decided to make an attempt to work on our relationship, things with us went from okay to a complete disaster. I tried to make it work over and over, but we were too gone. Throughout my pregnancy, I had come to realize his lies, immaturity, and deceitfulness.

He was apparently lying to me about where he was and seeing other girls. He cheated on me to the point I was scared because I was pregnant. I went to my OBGYN, and he said, "I was unfaithful, and she needs to be tested." There I was, embarrassed to the point that it had come to this after I gave him the option to walk away. Now, I was more concerned about getting tested for STDs for my baby's safety. Everything came out negative, thank God, but it was the point that I could never fully trust him. His treatment and actions towards me were unforgivable, and I could not let go of his deceit. The damage done to our relationship was irreparable.

As for my baby, I was told by my doctor that I would be given 50/50 chance to carry my daughter to term. I declined to test for down-syndrome and amniocentesis testing. At that point, it didn't matter what any test revealed. I was going to love the baby no matter what. I loved the baby from the moment I found out she was coming, and I would do anything in my power to keep her safe.

Jessica M. Brewer

MOTHERHOOD

In February 2004, I gave birth to a beautiful baby girl. From the moment I laid my eyes on her, my heart was filled with so much love. I ended up having a C-section to deliver her. I vividly remember the day I felt her turn breach. Philip was driving me back to my parent's house to drop me off, and we got into an argument about his infidelity. He stopped the truck in the middle of the road while it was heavily snowing out and made me walk home. I was 8 months pregnant at the time. One of my friends stopped and told me to get in their Chevy Blazer and drove me home.

That night I was so upset. That's when it happened—my mother literally saw her do a complete turn in my stomach. Shortly after that, I went to the doctor and found out she was breach and stuck under my ribs. I also discovered that my placenta was ripping away from my uterus. I delivered earlier than my due date because it could have taken my life and my unborn child's if I hadn't.

I continually dealt with Philip's high level of immaturity, and I became more and more distant. I found out that he was expecting another child from another woman. I kicked him out of my house and never looked back. I had built a 20-foot brick wall around my heart. My emotions were on lock-down, and I promised myself that no one could ever enter my life again and make me feel so worthless. Evil is a wind that blows no good deed. Despite the time I wasted and the hurt I experienced in that relationship, one great thing that came out of it was my beautiful, healthy baby girl.

When she was born, though my relationship with her father was unstable, and I was on an unending emotional roller coaster, I promised both myself and her that I would do anything to support her. She was my precious rock. I love her with everything I have.

***

I decided when she was a year old to go back to college and finish up my degree. I started back at Jefferson Community College to finish what I started. During that period, I experienced the toughest situations with Philip. I had to put an end to the mental and physical abuse. We were separated, and I just didn't want any part of that life—the fighting and arguing—anymore. But he wouldn't leave me alone, and I wanted him in the worst way to stop harassing me and let me live my life. I didn't want to keep filing papers for court based on harassment because I thought that maybe one day, he will realize that he had to move on.

Philip had a temper. He would show up at my house and drive through my yard leaving ruts in the grass. He kicked in my front door on numerous occasions. The deck that was built for my front door was all torn apart when I came home from work. I had to put a stop to this reckless behavior. I didn't want my daughter to see this and later on think that it was normal for her dad to do the things he did. I finally had to get an Order of Protection against him to stop harassing me. So, I got an Order of Protection stating that he could contact me, but he has to refrain from harassment.

My parents were always there to help clean up his mess. My dad had to fix the porch so Jaylynn and I could get into the house. He also had to fix my front door so it would lock. There were so many inexplicable and unforgivable acts committed by Philip that I would not accept that way of life for Jaylynn. I wanted to protect her.

He even went so far as to spread rumors about me to ensure that nobody would want to get involved with me. I heard that I took his house, even though my parents paid for the house and I paid them back. He said that I cheated all the time on him, which I did not. I realized that I had to come to terms with knowing his childhood and how he was brought up. I felt bad for him, but only *he* could change *his* ways. I couldn't change him.

I had to decide the type of mother I wanted to be for my daughter. I had to decide if I wanted to expose her to the dysfunction that was my relationship with her father or do I want her to be in a stable, loving environment. I decided that she deserved everything that I could give to her.

I kept her from as many negative situations as I could, but some things I couldn't protect her from. Her father would schedule visitations but then not show up, or he would have an excuse as to why he couldn't come and spend time with her. It happened on many occasions, so eventually, I didn't even tell her that her father was coming unless he was at my door. The disappointment in her eyes, along with the tears, was enough to make me better and stronger for her.

I didn't mind being a father and mother during that time. I would rather her stay with me anyways because of his track record. I wanted her safe. I was just hoping that someday he would be aware of and acknowledge how the negative things he has done has affected her. I have tried and still continue to try to this day to explain to him how his broken promises and absence has negatively impacted her. She is beginning to understand that he is not spending time with her. All she wanted was him to pay attention to her and be a father figure.

My father was always the one she cherished the most. He was a great role model for her and the only consistent male figure that she had to look up to. My dad always loved seeing her smile, and she loves her papa. He has taught her many great things, funny things. He created a monster; she was spoiled.

She always had fun when she visited her Mema and Papa's house. Dad and my daughter would always play pranks in an attempt to scare one another. He would walk into the living room as she would jump out from the stairs, and my dad would spill his beer down his shirt. Or, he would teach her to drive the big four-wheeler and come back wet with mud all over the place.

My father also taught her how to plant a garden. She got so excited to go over there to water it and check and see if anything was growing. She loved helping Mema and Papa with whatever they needed. Whether it's working on the pool with Mema during the summer or helping Papa with the wood in the fall, she absolutely loves her grandparents. She has spent her childhood years in that house. That was her stable, loving environment that provided a place for us to feel safe from the outside world.

During all the setbacks and the roller coaster ride with my ex, I managed to better myself. I got my degree, majoring in Paralegal Studies with a minor in Criminal Justice. I was completely shocked by how I overcame so much to make our lives better in an effort to support my beautiful daughter. I focused on just Jaylynn and me. I studied hard in the books while working every day going to night school.

***

I wouldn't have done it without everyone who helped me along the way, especially Aunt Mary and Aunt Debbie. Aunt Mary was Jaylynn's first babysitter. Because United Technologies was shutting down all buildings and moving production, I received severance pay in 2005 and had to find another job.

I started working at Pulaski Ford and Mercury as a service advisor. Aunt Mary took Jaylynn in and watched her so I could go back to work. I missed so much of her first, but it was a sacrifice I had to make to be a provider for us both.

When I did get home, Jaylynn would be excited to

tell me about her day. Aunt Mary would detail all of it the next morning to me. She knew I would want to be the first to hear about Jaylynn's milestones, and she kept up with every single one in detail.

I respected and appreciated her for allowing me the opportunity to hear about her firsts since I was not there when they occurred. But I can honestly say that Jaylynn surprised me with things no one would ever enjoy as much as I did. I can remember we were outside planting flowers, and she fell.

"Mommy, I need bandaid. I got boo boo!" she said to me.

"Aww, baby, it's ok. It's a little scratch."

After a few minutes of consoling her, I say, "Ok, honey! Go inside, mommy will be in, in a minute."

So, she goes inside as I finished up. I go inside to check on her, and as I am walking down to my room, she comes out of my master bathroom.

"Mommy, I got boo boo's all over!" she exclaimed.

I immediately start laughing. "Baby, you sure do!" She came walking out with my feminine panty liners stuck to her all over her body—on her forehead, cheeks, and in her hair. Apparently, she thought those bandaids were the bomb, but little did she know that someday she is not going to think that those bandaids were going to be the cat's meow. I tried to explain to her that those were for mommy's big boo boo every month. I seriously thought it was the most precious moment. Even though I missed a lot, I ended up with a lot of the first special moments overall.

I was still in the midst of finalizing my layoff from United Technologies Carrier. In addition to receiving a severance package, I also was eligible for unemployment and went back to school. Aunt Mary helped by watching her at nights so that I could take night classes. She helped me in any way she could.

One day, Aunt Mary came up to me to have a conversation.

"I need to talk to you for a minute."

"Ya, Aunt Mary, what's going on?"

"Mark and I are moving to Utica to live with Matthew, and we will be moving in a month. I wanted to tell you that I talked with my sister Debbie, and she is willing to take Jaylynn if you're interested in her watching her for you?"

"I didn't expect to hear that, but I am glad that you

told me. I am going to miss you, and I know Jaylynn is going to miss you more because she is attached to you and her little friends."

"It's really hard for me because this is all I've ever known, and it's going to be really difficult for me." She started to cry, and all I could do is give her a huge hug.

"We are going to miss you, Aunt Mary. You will always be in our hearts. Please stop crying because you're going to make me cry like a baby."

We both started smiling. "Don't worry, we will see you again," I assured her.

"You got that right!" She continued to tell me again that she was devastated to let her daycare kids go, but her sister, Aunt Debbie, was able to watch Jaylynn for me.

Aunt Debbie was amazing. She has been watching kids for many years. She would only watch her family members' children. All her nieces, nephews, and cousins just loved Aunt Debbie. She helped me many times while I had to work on the weekends and while I was in school. I was thankful that she was flexible for me. As an added bonus, I loved her baking. I would always look forward to her chocolate chips cookies and her Avon Bingo.

We also got support from Aunt Kylee because she was there to help my daughter and I get through the nonsense that came along with her brother Philip. Aunt Kylee loved her niece and that was never going to change. My daughter loves spending time with her aunt and her cousins, Tyler, Chase, and Sissy. Aunt Kylee is the only member of her father's family that calls her frequently and makes sure she is loved.

She is the only one in that family that is willing to go out of her way for my daughter. She takes my daughter to camp all the time, takes her to go get her hair done, and even takes her shopping. I love her, her two boys, and her mom, Donna, to pieces. I am proud to know that they will always be there for my daughter and provide her with the family she deserves.

***

As the days went on, I realized that making her happy was all I needed in my life. I didn't need to be in a relationship to make me happy or to make her happy. I was fine without it. All I needed to do was find a way to occupy my time. So, for peace of mind, I continued to play softball every Tuesday night during the summer and cards every Thursday.

In addition to my personal life and own recreational activities, I was very involved in my daughter's activities. I coached my daughter's softball team for a couple of years; my sister and brother in law ran APW Little League. It was a fantastic program for the kids, and I was very much involved in helping my sister and her husband. All the Little League fields were located in Williamstown. This enabled me to stop and see Joe's sister, Jessica.

One day, I was coaching my daughter's team and ran into Joe. I never thought in a million years that the one man for whom I always cared for deeply would enter my life again. We talked on many occasions, and finally, he asked me to go with him to his grandparents' 50th wedding anniversary party. I thought that was nice of him.

Of course, the family loved the idea that I was coming with him. I remember meeting him at a bar called Happy Valley Inn before the party started to grab a drink and talk. We had a great conversation reminiscing and laughing about moments together.

I asked Joe, "Do you remember about when you took the four-wheeler at Toby's house and didn't see the ditch and went flying into the road? The next day you had a black eye and a concussion?"

"Ya, my head felt like jello. I could sink my finger into the side of my head."

I just laughed because sometimes he was just overdramatic, but it was funny how he described things.

"Do you remember picking glass out of my shoulders when I broke Jason's light with the nunchucks?" he asked.

I busted out laughing, almost spitting out the beer I just took a sip out of. "Of course, amongst other things."

We continued to talk about all the good times we shared. We realized we had a lot of history together. I never thought I could open my heart to anyone again, but for some reason, he had a way to make all the pain that I was suffering go away in an instant. All the fears and negativity that would creep in my head were gone when I was with him.

The event took place at the reception hall in Camden, New York. It was Joe's Grandparents' 50th Anniversary Party. We sat at the same table with Joe's cousins—Kirk, Joelon, and their girlfriends. His sister Jessica also sat with us. We all sat at the table, joking around with everyone. Joe was the type of person that would strike a conversation about something that no one would ever talk about. We sat there looking at Joe, saying, "Only you, Joe."

Joe had a personality that would make anyone love him. He wouldn't have to say anything; he could just make a funny face, and everyone would die laughing to the point where we would be crying or peeing our pants. Right then and there, I realized how much I missed him.

That night, we said our goodbyes after the party and went our separate ways. He called the next day and said he wanted to talk to me. He confessed to all the things he had done not only to me but to my parents as well. It was shocking, but it allowed me to make my peace with the situation. I decided that I could continue to see him and forgive him for his past transgressions.

As time went on, Philip found out I was seeing someone. As expected, like he has done with everyone else, he tried to drive them out of my life by making up horrible stories about me. But Joe was smart; he knew what kind of person I was and who I had become. He stood up to my daughter's father to keep him from mentally abusing me and to keep him away from both Jaylynn and me. I can remember Philip showing up at my house, yelling at me and pushing me. I finally had enough, and I pushed back, and Philip punched me in the face.

I called Joe, and he took me to Urgent Care for x-rays because I thought Philip broke my eye socket. Joe was furious and called him and said, "Man, what are you doing? Do you understand what your consequences are? You're not only hurting yourself, but you're hurting your own daughter because of what you keep on doing."

"What the hell do you know?" spat Philip before he hung up on Joe. Eventually, he threatened Joe and I because he could not take the fact of me possibly moving on with my life whatsoever.

Joe decided that I needed to control my life and get a restraining order because Philip was out of control. Then and there, Joe told me that we should take a break for a little bit until I could get a restraining order to protect my daughter and me from her father.

I was sad, but I completely understood where he was coming from. He told me that he would always be there for me if I needed him, but before we could settle down, I needed Philip to understand boundaries. Why would I bring Joe into my life when I have an uncontrollable ex-boyfriend that constantly tries to interfere with anything I do? Talk about possessive.

The last straw was when I had to call the cops on him for an incident that happened in Altmar at a gas station. Philip bought a Camaro just like mine and used to follow me all over the place. This time, he showed up to Little Lukey's with his girlfriend and wanted to take my daughter. As he was trying to pry her out of my arms, I was screaming for help. He had pulled the nozzle out of my Camaro and sprayed gas all over my car and my legs.

I called the police to report the incident, then I called Joe and said, "Philip and his girlfriend showed up to Little Lukey's, and he wanted to take Jaylynn, and it wasn't his visitation. Can you please bring me my Durango and swap vehicles with me? He sprayed gas all over my car."

"Ok, I will be right there!" Joe showed up while I was giving my statement to the police officers.

The officer said, "You know at this point we have to arrest him, right?"

"Yes, this was the last straw," I said calmly. He could have hurt us. I am done with the harassment."

"Now, this is public record," explained the officer, "So, you can go to the courthouse on Monday and get a complete stay away restraining order."

"I have an order of protection, but we can still have verbal conversations. I need an order for him to completely stay away from me."

"He needs to have a wake-up call before he really hurts someone."

"Trust me, I already know," I agreed.

"I need a phone number to get in touch with him right now." I gave the officer Philip's phone number, and he called him right away.

The officer told Philip, "You need to turn yourself in, or I will put a warrant out for your arrest. I am warning you right now to completely stay away from Jessica and her residence. If you plan on seeing your kid, then you better straighten yourself out."

Philip said things to the officer and pretty much hung up on him. Joe told the officer that he called Philip after I had called him to come get my car and said that he wouldn't listen to Joe either. The look on

Joe's face when he looked at me was unexplainable. I knew that he needed to take a step away from the situation before it got worse. I thought he would protect me and make me feel safe from him. We could have gotten hurt; Philip never thought about his actions.

The next day, the police report of Philip's arrest was on the front page of the newspaper. Everyone in my town knew what had happened. I wasn't one to bring my personal life out and in the open, but that's when I hit rock bottom again.

Side note: I was going to start a new job at the Child's Advocate Office, a county job with full benefits. However, because I called the police for domestic abuse, they rescinded the job offer and said that I was no longer suitable for the position.

***

I cried my eyes out on many occasions because Philip ruined so many great things in my life. I never thought that Joe walking away from me would be so devastating. We were even talking about getting married and having children of our own. Joe expressed how he was so happy that we finally made our way back to each other and how we were meant to be together. I was shocked that all those conversations and moments we spent together were going to be no more. We continued to talk once in a while after. I thought that at some point, we would be back together because we began having those same conversations.

I never expected to get a phone call at 7 a.m. to tell me the love of my life was gone. Tammy called me and said, "Jess?" I could hear her crying, and she couldn't catch her breath.

"Hey, Tammy, what's wrong?"

"There has been an accident!"

"What do you mean an accident, Tammy? What is going on? Tell me!"

"Joe crashed his bike this morning around 3 a.m., and he didn't make it!!"

She was crying, telling me that the love of my life was gone! It didn't register with me at first.

"Joe hit a utility pole and didn't make it," she repeated.

"No!" I screamed. "That's not possible! There is no way!"

"Jess, you need to come to Williamstown and find Jessica and Darlene!" My knees crashed to the floor in my bedroom, and my heart dropped. Tears were rolling down my face trying to make sense of everything. I didn't want to believe it for one second. I tried calling Joe, begging him to call me back, telling him that I loved him because I never told him during the time we spent together. No answer. I called again and again. Leaving message after message and no answer. I tried reaching out to his family, but no one was answering their phones.

So, I asked my sister to take my daughter so I could go to his mom's house. When I arrived at my sister's house, she opened the door and burst into tears.

"Jess," she said between sobs. "He *is* gone. I am so sorry." She grabbed me to keep me from passing out. I still couldn't believe it. My body was in complete and utter shock. I was supposed to live the rest of my life with this guy that I absolutely loved and cherished. Why is everyone telling me he's gone? I gathered myself, said bye to my daughter, and drove in a fog. I didn't even remember the drive to the Town of Williamstown. I was determined to prove everyone wrong. He was probably at Kirk and Joelon's house passed out sleeping.

As I was driving up to the Town of Osceola, I passed his mom's vehicle. Quickly, I turned around to follow them. They pulled over, saying they were heading to Bumpy's house—Joe's grandparents. We waited for some time, not knowing what to think.

When the coroner called, I lost my mind. I cried in disbelief that this was happening. I remember his mom and Jessica had to go identify the body, and when they returned, we knew that it was true. He was gone. I never felt so empty; it was as though someone had torn my heart right out of my chest! I couldn't breathe, and my eyes were so swollen from the crying that they were practically shut. *My life is over,* I thought to myself. I felt incomplete.

The day of his funeral was the toughest day of my life. So many people paid their respects. Joe was loved by everyone. I met people that knew me as Joe's girl that I had never met before. Everyone knew who I was and said sorry for my loss. I can remember his aunt framing a picture that was taken not too long before that on Easter of the three of us, and she presented it to me at the funeral.

I lost my mind and couldn't stop crying. It was a long day. I can remember it pouring rain at first, and immediately after, the sun came out and was as bright as can be. I knew that Joe was giving us all a sign saying that he was crying but wanted everyone to know that he was ok. I can remember a bird pooping on Charlie's shirt, and we knew it was Joe making his presence known. Even in heaven, he was cracking jokes.

After a long day of crying and everything I had been through, I told myself that I would never be hurt again. From that moment on, I shut off my feelings towards many different things in life. I showed my love to my daughter every day, but I put myself to the side and focused on her. I was her mother, so I wanted to make sure she had the life she deserved. It took me a long time to get over all the sadness I had in my life throughout the years. One thing I knew I was good at was being a dedicated and loving mother.

***

After I finally graduated from college, I had a graduation party to celebrate my success and invited all of Joe and I's family and friends. We all needed to be together and have a distraction. In the back of everyone's mind, we all were still mourning our loss. It took me over a year to pull myself together and for the vivid dreams and nightmares of Joe to stop. Sometimes I felt that he was sending me a message.

It felt so real—like he was still alive right there with me.

As time went on, I realized again that God will only give you what you can handle in life and that everything happens for a reason. I was so desperate to find that reason so I could heal my wounds.

***

So many years passed by. I dated here and there, but I never found exactly who I was looking for. I fell in love with the idea of dating an older man with two children. It was great, but I knew that he wouldn't put up with my ex's issues. Plus, he knew the heartache I went through. His sister, Donna, told him about me, plus we had mutual friends. We had a lot of fun together. We both played softball together. It was great that we both shared the same interests, but most importantly, we both adored our children. I knew he was a great man and father, and this is what attracted me to him. He was supportive in the beginning, but things faded in time.

Fun fact: I was working at a law firm as a paralegal when we first met, and I ran for Sandy Creek Town Justice. I thought for sure I would have won my election. I ran as a candidate for the Republican Party, and I got enough signatures from the people that lived in the town to run as an Independent as well. The girl that won was the judge's secretary of that court. I lost by a few votes. I was bummed, but at least I had given it a try.

During the campaign, I had a lot of help from his parents and my own. I thought our relationship was going to be forever, but things drifted after I found out I had skin cancer. I also began to have heart palpitations. I had to start wearing a heart monitor because the palpitations became more frequent. I wanted him to be understanding, and I realized I needed someone by my side more than ever.

Unfortunately, he was not the person for me. Not to mention he couldn't have any more children and that right there was enough to walk away. I guess it just made it easier for me. It was a great three years, but then again, it wasn't *exactly* what I wanted in life. I wanted to get married and have more children. In January 2011, we both called it quits. At the age of 33, I gave up that dream after we split up because I was getting older and who would ever want me at that age? Time proved to me that I was wrong.

***

I sold my house and moved in with my parents so they could take care of me. While I was trying to overcome skin cancer and undergoing treatment, I was still working at Red Lobster. I had quit my paralegal job at the law firm because the attorney I worked for got mad, threw a lamp across the room, and was kicking chairs. He was not very professional, and that was the last straw. I had to get my stuff and get out of there.

I got hired at Red Lobster in Spring 2010. I was still working at Red Lobster waitressing, and it was hard because I was tired every day and not feeling well. My bosses, Brian and Staci, were amazing people. They cared and understood what I was enduring. All my co-workers were a great group of people to work with. I was shocked that they had arranged a fundraiser to help support me and my daughter during that difficult time. I had to take a leave of absence because I was extremely stressed, and I needed to focus on my health and get my life back on track.

As time went on, I got the care I needed and had overcome the fear of leaving my daughter on this earth alone. I had an aggressive form of skin cancer and was thankful that it was taken care of by amazing doctors. Still, to this day, I have a biopsy occasionally to make sure that I am clean from melanoma.

I had a hard time getting back to normal, and I wanted to continue my career as a paralegal. I knew that I couldn't waitress anymore and that I had to focus on a Monday through Friday, 40 hour a week position because it was more stable for Jaylynn and me.

I was finally hired at a law firm I loved working for, but I was still missing something in my life. I felt that I was just going through the motions every day. I was content but still not where I wanted to be in life. I was ok with that because I was raising the most beautiful girl in the world on my own. My mom suggested that I go on some dating websites to try and find happiness for myself. I can remember her saying to me, "Jess, you're not getting any younger, honey, maybe you should try it out and see where it goes."

I went on some dates, but none of the men were really acknowledging the fact that I had a daughter. It was a red flag on most dates, and I wasn't happy about how they reacted when I told them I had a little girl. It would raise red flags when I would ask my dates what their long-term goals are or what they are looking for in a relationship, and they couldn't give me answers. It seemed like they weren't ready for a long-term relationship or a commitment with my daughter and me. I knew what I wanted in my life, and I wasn't going to settle for anything less.

One red flag I had was pretty funny because I definitely caught my first catfish. For example, I went on a date with a guy that was wearing skinny jeans. He looked manly, but the sound of his voice was feminine. I met him at a Chinese restaurant and just from the first impression, I was ready to leave. I literally went to the bathroom and called my mother. I called her and said, "Mom! I need you to help me out and get me out of this date. I feel like I found my first catfish. I will explain later."

"Geez, Jess. What do you want me to do?"

"Call me in about 10 minutes and just tell me to come home or just sit on the phone. Ok?"

"Whatever, Jess," she chuckles. "I will call you!"

"Thanks, mom," I praised. "You're the best!"

She did what I asked, and I made it seem like I had to leave right away.

My mother thought I was extremely picky by not giving anyone the time of day; she was right. I have been burned and hurt so much that I was not going to settle for anything less than what I wanted in my life for both my daughter and me. I mean come on; we *are* a packaged deal.

LOVE AT FIRST SIGHT

One of the best days of my life was when I finally met my soul mate. I happened to start talking to this guy named Casey who was in the United States Military and stationed in Fort Drum, New York. It is only 45 minutes from where I lived. I was skeptical because he was younger than I was—like 11 years younger than me. Our conversations by text were amazing. It seemed like a dream come true because he was polite, caring, and knew how to express himself. We exchanged some pictures and got acquainted.

From the start, he would always text me in the morning and say, "Good morning, beautiful." It was always a great start to my day seeing those texts. It made me feel special, but in the back of my mind, I was hesitant. I felt that it was going to be another disappointment. I mentioned to my mother about meeting this guy and asked her if I should go or not. In case you didn't notice, every date I went on, I would tell her about.

"How will you ever know if you don't go?" she asked as she took a swig of her drink. "So, what if he is younger than you, just go and enjoy yourself and have a great dinner."

"I guess I will go," I agreed. "It's not hurting anything." I could already feel that I was extremely attracted to him, and I hadn't even met him yet. I was eager to meet him, but I was also nervous about my feelings and how to express them because, to be quite frank, my heart had been on lockdown for a long time. I guess I was scared to fall in love with someone that I had feelings for because I just refused to get hurt. I didn't want to open the gate to my heart at all.

The day that I was going to meet Casey was nerve-wracking. I wanted work to be over. The day dragged on and on; it felt like it was never going to end. After work, I went home to shower and get ready for our first date. It was a beautiful day in the summer, so I decided to wear a sleeveless ruffle black dress. Casey was just getting off work and told me that he would meet me at Moe's parking lot. After that, we decided where we wanted to go for dinner.

As I was driving up Route 81, I was so nervous because he was so handsome. I had so many thoughts running through my mind. *What if he doesn't like me because I am older than him? Is this going to be another catfish situation?* At the time, I was a smoker, so I chained smoked all the way up there to meet him.

When I get there, he's nowhere in sight. *Here we go, another letdown,* I thought. Just when I was about to give up, he calls me and tells me he's on Route 781 and will be right there. I watched him pull into the parking lot, and he got out of a Black SUV. As he rounds the back of the car, we look at each other for the first time with pure excitement. He was tall and handsome, with blonde hair and blue eyes—in short, he was a sexy man.

Within seconds, he grabbed me, embraced me in a hug, and lifted me off the ground. I wrapped my legs around him as he kissed my lips. I didn't think he would ever let me down. It just seemed like we knew each other forever and that we hadn't seen one another in a long time. It felt so…natural. The feeling of being wanted was incredible. The vibes rolling off him made me feel relaxed and very comfortable. He looked at me like nobody has ever looked at me. I couldn't believe the connection we had.

After we got out of our daze, we decided that we wanted to go to Taco Bell then find a place to talk and get to know one another. We parked in a parking lot and talked about our jobs and every other topic you could think of. We had our first real kiss, sparks were flying, and fireworks were popping off. His sweet soft lips were tender as they brushed mine. I don't think either one of us could keep our hands off each other.

He had an idea that we would go to a motel and get a room to spend more time with each other. I agreed, and let me just say that it was a night I will never forget. I will forever hold it close to my heart. Our deep conversations were heartfelt, and I knew that he was looking to find his special lady as I was looking to find my handsome man. He knew I had a daughter and was completely excited about it because he loved kids.

Casey told me that he wanted to get married and have children, which was exactly what I wanted. He kept telling me how beautiful I was and that he was shocked that I was 34 years old at the time. He did not care about my age and told me that I looked younger than I was. But it didn't stop there. Things got heated, and I can remember standing by the window, looking at the beautiful neon pink sunset while he came from behind me and wrapped his arms around my waist.

"Isn't that so beautiful?" I whispered.

"Yes, as beautiful as you!"

"I feel like this is meant to be. I never felt like this!"

"I agree with you," he said as he held me tighter. "It feels natural, and it feels so good." Right then and there, I was falling at his feet. It was a feeling that

I never ever had, filled with happiness and security. He made me feel safe in his arms. Neither one of us wanted to leave each other that night. I did have to ask him if he wanted to see me again in person because, like I said, it felt too good to be true.

"I have to be honest with you and ask you a question?" I said to him seriously.

"What is it?"

"Do you want to see me again after tonight?"

I can remember him looking at me and saying, "Definitely, yes. It would be my honor to take you out and spend more time with you!"

"I would love to see you again too!"

"Well, you're not getting rid of me already?"

"No!" I giggled. "Absolutely not!"

Our time that evening came to an end, and he asked me to text him when I got home, so he knew I was safe. I never had anyone ask me that before. From there, I knew he was a caring man. As I was on my way home, I had so many thoughts running through my head, thinking I found my soul mate. It was love at first sight, but I didn't want to scare him away with my thoughts and feelings. I wanted to make sure that we were still on the same page.

During our talk the first night, I told him, "I want to be completely honest with you. I don't want to hold back my feelings because I have been through a lot in my life. I am asking you not to lead me on because it wouldn't be fair to either of us if you did."

"Why would I lead you on? I want to see you again! I feel the same way about you, and I hope you feel the same about me. I don't want to hurt you. I want to settle down and get married. I want to start a family. I don't want my time wasted either."

"Good because I really like you, and I don't want to waste any more time in my life."

"You're amazing, and I would love for you to be a part of my life."

As the conversations continued, he made it very clear to me that he wanted to see more of me and that he wanted to meet my daughter. I told him that he wouldn't meet her until I knew it was the right time. He completely understood, but he was anxious to meet her.

I've always prided myself on never bringing men

in and out of her life. I kept my personal life secret from her. I didn't want to expose her to behavior that is not morally right. Casey was patient with me. He knew that I was protecting her interests and saw that my love for her was greater than anything else in the world.

The more and more we talked, we knew that we shared the same feeling towards one another. We both had feelings that ran so deep that we could not bear to be separated. We talked about him meeting my parents and my daughter as well.

One Saturday morning in September, I told my parents about my feelings for Casey and that he wanted to meet them.

"Mom," I said dreamily. "I feel like I have met my soul mate. I just can't explain the feelings that I have for him."

"See, and you didn't want go out with him because of his age and now look at you!" she smiled.

"I know, Mom. I was just nervous because he was 11 years younger than me."

"Age is just a number, and if you're happy, who cares how old he is."

"You're right, Mom. I haven't been this happy in a long time."

"Believe me, I see it. Your daughter sees it and your dad sees it. We are happy for you!"

"Thanks, Mom, for changing my mind that night because if it wasn't for you, then I would not have gone."

"I am glad you went and had fun. I can't wait to meet him," she added. She was thrilled to invite him to a spaghetti dinner. I told her that I will ask him when he would be able to come out. So, we planned for him to come and meet everyone. I was both nervous and scared. I hoped that this would be our next step towards the future. I was hoping that I could be his girl and he my man for the rest of our lives.

***

It was a Sunday afternoon when he came for dinner. I drove up to Fort Drum to get him because he didn't have a vehicle of his own. As soon as we walked through the door to the kitchen, my dad came out first to greet Casey, and my mother was close behind him. They were happy to introduce themselves to the man I was falling head over heels for.

As my dad was talking to him, my little munchkin came flying out of the living room to meet Casey. I can remember the sparkle he had in his eye meeting her for the first time. Of course, she wanted to show him her toys or whatever she was doing at the time. He fell in love with her smile and her sense of humor.

We sat down in the living room so my parents could get to know him more. I leaned back and soaked up the conversation. I can see that my father was impressed by how Casey was so polite and respectful. My dad asked him if he wanted a beer, and Casey said that he would never turn down an invite of having a beer with him.

My mother fed us at the table, and Casey was so thankful for his dinner because he didn't get home-cooked meals at all. I can remember the gigantic bowl of spaghetti my mother made for Casey, and I couldn't believe that he devoured most of it. I guess he *was* a growing man, after all.

After dinner, Casey expressed his sincere appreciation for my parents having him over. My mom gave him a hug and told him that he was always welcome into her house. It was great to know that she already accepted him into the family, and I think Casey knew it too. I think by the look in both of our eyes, we knew our relationship was going to progress into something special. As the conversation went on and we shared laughs, I knew that he was a keeper.

The most interesting part of the evening was when our neighbor veered off-road by our house and hit the trees as he was going around the curve. It was so loud that we heard the crash inside our house. My father and Casey ran outside to see what had happened. There was our neighbor saying he didn't have any brakes in the car, and it wouldn't slow down. Our neighbor was on the phone trying to get the car up the road to Harold's abandoned house.

Meanwhile, Harold came flying up the road in his minivan so fast, I thought he was going to run us over. Harold is one comical man who is always there to lend a hand. He would take the shirt off his back to help anyone. He always says to all the women, "Where have you been all my life" as he smiles and gives them a hug.

So, that was the night he met Casey for the first time. I introduced Harold to Casey, and they shook hands. They had a little conversation and then discussed how to get the car up the road to Harold's house. Casey volunteered to get in the car and steer while Harold towed it up the road. As they were towing it, sparks were flying left and right. At that moment, I thought the car was going to catch on fire. I was screaming up the road to stop, but no one could hear me. The last thought in my mind was that the car was going to explode because it was leaking gas and oil.

Luckily, they got the car up there with no issues. Dad and I were standing at the edge of the road watching Casey walk toward us.

"I was scared for your life!" I cried as he started getting closer to me.

"I'm perfectly fine," shrugged Casey. "You worry too much. I grew up on a farm, and this is nothing."

I guess I should have taken that as a sign of relief, but my heart was still ready to jump out of my chest. When we all go back inside, my father starts walking towards the fridge.

"I think it's time for another beer," he said to Casey.

"I couldn't agree more."

While we were talking about the events of the evening, Jaylynn was eager to get Casey's attention to play with her. That's when he got on the floor and started to tickle her. Jaylynn was a jokester, and I swear she can copy the voice of anyone. As she was torturing him and he was tickling her, she was making Casey laugh with all the different voices she mimicked. At one point, he was tickling her so bad that I thought she was going to pee her pants. At that very moment, I knew I was falling in love with him. For a guy to accept not only me but my daughter as well? Yeah, that turned my whole outlook on finding happiness around.

What I was receiving was a gift. God was giving me the opportunity to love again. For the past few years, I had lived my life with a wall built to block all my emotions to prevent me from getting hurt. The hurt and all the disappointments I had throughout the years seemed to no longer matter. Casey was breaking my walls down piece by piece. He was opening my heart up with every word spoken and every gesture he made from the day I met him. I realized that God finally sent me my soul mate.

My mom told me one day that Joe was watching over me, and he saw the life I had lived and sent Casey to cross paths with me. She knew that Joe wanted me to be happy. I felt that it was my time to enjoy happiness and possibly start a future with Casey and have a family.

We both knew that we loved each other from the first day we met. I didn't even mention my feelings because he literally took the words right out of my mouth every time. Each time he would profess his love to me, I would always reply that I felt the same way about everything he was feeling. I never felt luckier than I did after he entered my life.

Not only was he good to me, but he was good to my daughter too. He always wanted to take Jaylynn and me places, and the best part was that he never once asked me to get a babysitter for her so we could do things alone. Right there, it made us feel like a family. He always said that he "loved being with his girls." Sure, we would go do things alone when Jaylynn was with her biological father, but it didn't feel the same when she was not with us. In addition to spending family time with just the three of us, we spent time with our friends too.

One weekend I had a softball tournament, and I really wanted him to come watch me play. He said that he had a tattoo appointment that Saturday, but he could come after if he could get his buddy to bring him. I waited for him to call, but I couldn't get cell reception in Redfield. I started getting nervous that he might not show. He sent me pictures of his new tattoo while he was getting it done and said that he and his friend, Webb, were going to get a couple drinks together. I didn't hear from him at all after that. I was bummed.

Naturally, negative thoughts began to enter my mind, and I was ready to shut down. I continued to have fun with my co-ed team and drink like we always did at the Redfield tournament. The next day I tried calling and calling, but I got no response. I just gave up. Maybe he wasn't Mr. Perfect after all.

A couple of hours go by, and he finally calls me back and tells me he had an extremely rough night with Webb after getting his tattoo. Apparently, they ran into the Syracuse basketball team because Webb was trying to pick a fight with the tallest guy there. After Casey intervened and smoothed things over, he told them to excuse his friend.

When the guys from the basketball team found out they were military, they decided to buy them drinks all night. Afterward, Webb became MIA, and Casey couldn't find him. He slept in Webb's Chevy Tahoe until he got a tap on the window the next morning from the Syracuse Police. Casey explained the situation and finally found Webb in the VA hospital. I understood the situation, but I felt there was no excuse for him not to call me and let me know what was going on.

At that point, I had to see him and explain a couple of things about what I was feeling. So, I drove up to Fort Drum Military Base, picked him up, and took him to his favorite place, Texas Roadhouse. As we were ordering, we started to open up to each other.

"Look, Jess," he started. "I'm sorry. I was wrong for doing that to you."

"Well, Casey, I need to be honest with you. I felt insecure when you didn't contact me and tell me why you didn't show. You shouldn't tell me that you're going to come then not show up. I need you to be a man of your word." The waitress set down our drinks and scurried off. "If you want us to work," I continued, "You need to understand that communication is very important to me."

"You're absolutely right," he said as he looked into my eyes. "I'm sorry. It won't happen again."

"I forgive you, but I'm still upset about it," I admitted.

"I promise I will make it up to you."

I was relieved that he told me that because my

heart couldn't take anymore disappointments. I opened my heart to him about everything that I have been through in my life—from my friends dying, having Jaylynn, losing Joe, continuously being in failed relationships, then having skin cancer. I was doing everything I could possibly do to support and love my daughter the way she deserved to be loved.

I can remember the look he gave me when he said these words: "I will never hurt you or Jaylynn. I fell in love with the both of you, and I mean that."

My heart was racing and overflowing with joy. I was glad I found a man who can express his feelings and tell you exactly how he feels. I really respected him that we can communicate without having an argument. I loved the fact our relationship was flawless. Now, I couldn't *imagine* my life without him. Just something about him that made me a better person and a better mother.

My outlook on life was starting to change the more and more we were together. That is when we both completely made it official that I was his girl and he was my man. The extra security made me feel at ease instead of wondering what may happen in the future between us. I was overwhelmed with love and tenderness that he was always willing to give me.

Sometimes I didn't know how to take it because I was never shown that kind of love that he was providing not only to me but my daughter. He was willing to help me with Jaylynn every day that we were together like he was her father right from the start. This melted my heart in more ways than one.

***

On Labor Day weekend, in September 2013, Casey told me that he had some news.

"I'm getting ready to deploy," he said seriously.

I looked at him in disbelief because I didn't really know what that meant. "What does that mean?" I asked.

"I have to leave for 9 months to serve my country. The exact date of my deployment was up in the air. All I know is that I'm either leaving in late October or early November."

I felt a lump form in my throat. I was overcome with sadness because here we are starting our relationship, and now he was leaving us. He saw the tears threatening to fall from my eyes.

"I will be forever be yours," he assured me. "I would be thankful if you could wait for me because—"

"Of course, I will," I interrupted. "I will support you, no matter what."

Truthfully, I had no idea what to expect. I definitely could have used a book for dummies because I felt incompetent. He suggested that we not think about the short time we were about to have together but enjoy the time we do have together.

Every year, the Bristol's down the road from my parents have a get-together on Labor Day weekend. Everyone brings a dish to pass along with their choice of beer and drinks while we all play volleyball. It feels like a reunion of friends because you always enjoy seeing the people that you don't get to see or talk to often. Barb and Steve came and met Casey for the first time. They liked him immediately. They got along so great, and I can remember them both saying that Casey was a keeper and that they were both happy for me. We were having a great time at the party drinking, laughing, and playing volleyball.

Linda approached Casey, telling him that he looked like Channing Tatum and that she wanted a lap dance. She is a very funny woman. I love her humor. She had all of us in stitches laughing so hard. Then, that's when he told me that he was a male stripper in the past. Well, let's just say I was completely intrigued with the concept that my boyfriend may one day give me a lap dance.

I was skeptical of how the day was going to be because everyone that knew me knew that I had been single for a while and that I was extremely picky when it came to dating. When everyone saw that I brought someone to the party, they knew it was for real. The best part was that Casey was a natural. He made people laugh, and he talked to everyone like he knew them forever. I can remember sitting next to my mom watching everything transpire.

"He fits right in with all our friends," she observed. "It's great to see you smiling for the first time in a long time." She took a sip of her drink, then looked at me seriously. "Jess, I really like him, and look what he gives you. I know he cares about you a lot."

Before I could respond, Casey came over and sat by my mother. "What's up, Mom?" he grinned. I thought that was the coolest thing because my mother had told him to stop calling her ma'am and call her Mom. So, we were all bullshitting, and my dad came over to join the conversation. That's when Casey stood up and asked my dad if he could talk to him in private. I can remember it as if it were yesterday.

"Sure," said my dad, "Let me grab another beer." As they took a couple steps away from my mother and me, we could still hear them talking.

"Well, sir, I was hoping to get your blessing in marrying your daughter," said Casey in a low voice. I was shocked.

"You guys haven't known each other that long," said Dad.

"It doesn't matter. I know she's the one I want to spend the rest of my life with. There's no doubt in my mind. I'm in love with both Jess and Jaylynn."

"Well," sighed Dad. "You have my blessing. Jess has just been through a lot, and I don't want to see her get hurt. But I am happy that you're taking her away," he chuckled. That was my dad's way of saying that I wasn't getting any younger either. "I will say this," said Dad after sipping his beer. "I'm proud of the man you are. I really appreciate you stepping up to the plate and being there for my granddaughter because she deserves to have stability in her life by having a father figure there supporting her."

"I will always be there for her," said Casey proudly. "I'll be there for the both of them for as long as I live."

I think Dad was happy to hear Casey say that to him. In the process of the conversation, not only could my mother and I overhear bits and pieces, but others did too. They were all shocked and happy, just like me. They were probably wondering where this guy came from and how long had I been seeing him. I didn't care about any of that, and I really didn't care about the age difference. Apparently, he didn't either. At that moment, I knew he was my forever and wanted it to be known that I was his and only his.

***

The next morning, I had to find out if he was serious.

"Good morning, beautiful," he said as he watched me roll over to face him.

"Hey," I smiled. "Do you remember talking to my dad?"

He looked at me with a blank face. "Yyyeeesss, why?"

"I was just wondering if you meant what you said last night."

He looked at me dumbfounded. "Well, how much did you hear?" he asked.

"Pretty much everything."

He grinned and looked at me like no other man had ever looked at me. Like I was the only woman he had ever laid eyes on. "I meant it all," he said as he kissed my hand. "I want to marry you someday, and I want you to be my wife. I love you, and I love the fact that you are a strong independent woman. You're the one I've been looking for. You possess the qualities of a wife. You're a great mother, and we both want the same things out of life."

He touched my heart by being so sincere and opening his heart to me. I felt safe as he was holding me while we laid in my bed. I was getting all warm and fuzzy inside while looking him in the eyes. I knew that he meant every word, and I was happy to accept the fact that one day he would ask me to be his wife. I was definitely glowing with excitement.

As we got out of bed, we went downstairs and saw Dad making breakfast. Dad always made breakfast on Sundays for Jaylynn and me. After breakfast, I got in the shower. As I was washing my hair, Casey knocked and told me to hurry up because he had to go back to Fort Drum ASAP.

"There was a recall, and everyone has to report back to base," he explained. "Looks like I was supposed to be back there an hour ago, and you know it takes forty-five minutes to get back from here."

I hurried up and got out of the shower to get dressed so we could head out of the house.

"I'll drive," he said patiently, "Because I don't want you to get a ticket. But we need to hurry. I'm going to be in trouble for not being there on time to report."

I was starting to get nervous for him because this was the first I ever heard of such a thing. Apparently, a few soldiers got into trouble the night before. As a result, the unit had to report back and be accountable. We finally arrived on base and pulled into the barracks where he was living. He rushed and gave me a kiss, telling me that he would call me later. He literally jumped out of my Chevy Trailblazer and ran inside to change and report.

***

I didn't hear from him until that evening. Apparently, one soldier got into a fight at a bar, and another got a DWI.

"Yeah, I got smoked as punishment for being late," said Casey. All kinds of wild thoughts ran through my mind. I was thinking they put him in a gas chamber or something.

"It's going to be okay," I said, attempting to console him about getting smoked.

"Do you even know what that means?"

"No," I chuckled. "I thought it was a gas chamber or something."

He began to laugh hysterically. He laughed so hard that he couldn't talk to me or stop laughing. So now, I am *really* curious about what getting smoked could possibly mean.

"So, what does it mean?" I asked as he composed himself.

"*That* was a good one. I have to give you credit for that," he laughed.

"C'mon, Casey. Just tell me what it means."

"Baby, they tore my shit up and made me do push-ups and sit-ups and things like that until I was shaking and couldn't do anymore."

"Well, you got your sweat on and sweat out all that beer from last night," I said relieved. I loved to joke around and smile with him. He always makes me smile.

***

The days go by, and we weren't able to see each other. We waited for the weekends to finally arrive so that we could actually spend quality time together. I swear it seemed like the work week dragged on while the weekends came and went in a blink of an eye. Each and every moment we spent together, we did with Jaylynn.

One day, we took her to the movies to see the last Twilight movie, *Breaking Dawn: Part 2*. Casey had never seen any of the movies, but he wanted to watch what we wanted to watch. He was so easy going, and I loved how he was a simple man, easy to impress and to please. I was starting to think that there was something wrong with him because in any other relationship I ever had, there would always be fighting or arguing.

After the movie was over, we decided to do a little shopping. He wanted to go to Kay Jewelers for a gift for his mother. As he was looking around, I decided to look at rings while he was talking to a store representative. A salesperson greeted me and asked what I wanted to look at. Casey told me I should try on a few rings while he shopped. I looked at this one ring; it stood out to me because it looked like the Eiffel Tower. It was absolutely stunning! Casey came back over, looked at my finger, and agreed that the ring was beautiful; he loved it too.

I sat there for a little bit longer trying on different rings, but for some reason, he kept going back to that ring, saying it was beautiful like me. I couldn't help but agree that I loved it too after I tried on so many of them.

Casey was still undecided on what to get his mother, so Jaylynn and I decided to go to the Justice Store. I told Casey to meet us there when he was done. Jaylynn loved the Justice store, and every mall we visited, she had to find one. It was the "in" thing at school. After twenty minutes or so had passed, Casey finally met up with us.

"What did you get your mother?" I asked.

"I picked out a couple of pieces, but I'm not sure what she would like."

"I am sure she would love anything you get her."

By this time, Jaylynn was starving, so he told us that we were eating at the Melting Pot, a fondue restaurant where you actually cook your own food. Needless to say, it was an experience, and Jaylynn loved cooking her own food.

After we ate, it was time to drive up north to Fort Drum and drop Casey off. I was sad to see him leave us. I believed that he should be by my side every day. I missed him terribly when I wasn't with him. It was tough during the week when I never knew when I would hear from him because he wasn't allowed to have his phone during training out in the field or even during the classes he had to take. I would get nervous because I wouldn't hear from him at all. All kinds of thoughts would run through my head, and none of them were happy ones.

In my previous relationships, because of all the lying and cheating, I had become jaded and untrusting. I was still scared of getting hurt. Casey was different, though. He was completely honest with me about everything, and I was completely honest with him too. I told him one night that I thought he was dating someone else. He was would constantly reassure me that I was the only one he wanted. It was great to hear that from him when I needed to hear it.

I loved the way that he would always make me feel secure, and I especially loved the way he was with

Jaylynn. I believe she felt it too. It was crazy at first because she would go to him and ask him for stuff before she would ask me. It kind of shocked me that she depended on him now more than me. I was elated that she was comfortable and loved him too.

I remember Casey made Jaylynn this yellow cord bracelet, and she would never take it off. When she did and couldn't find it, she cried and cried for it. It was actually adorable how much she loved that bracelet and how much she looked up to Casey. She adored him like he was her own father. She would stick to him like peanut butter does to jelly.

***

Back to back weekends, I had two weddings to attend. One was my previous neighbor's daughter, and the other was my best friend, Scotty's wedding. As both weddings were approaching, I had asked Casey if he would be able to attend them with me. He said yes, but he didn't have anything to wear.

So, we had to go do a little bit of shopping the weekend before. I picked him up and decided that we would go to JCPenney to find him a pair of slacks and a dress shirt. He gives me his pants size, a 34. So, I grabbed a pair of size 34 pants, never paying attention to the length because I never had to shop for men's pants before. He is in the dressing room, and I handed him a pair of black slacks.

As I continue to look for different slacks, he yells my name and comes out of the dressing room with the pants on looking just like Urkel. The pants were so tight I could literally see the outline of his genitals. I started laughing so hard because he made it so obvious that he didn't care who saw him looking like a complete and utter nerd strutting around in those slacks.

Jaylynn came running towards us, showing me the shirt she found for Casey. He starts to run back into the dressing room, but he couldn't get the pants off. He called me in to tug on the pant legs so he could finally get out of the slacks. Then he clues me in about the proper length that he wears. We are both ready to pee our pants because we are laughing so hard.

Jaylynn is a nosey one. Naturally, her curiosity was piqued when she saw us laughing uncontrollably. She wants to know why we are both laughing so hard. I had to tell her that Casey was wearing the wrong size pants and looked like Urkel, the nerd. When she saw him, she began laughing and picked on Casey about him looking like a nerd. My stomach hurt so bad after that whole situation that I couldn't even eat my dinner.

The first wedding was in Central Square at the golf course, and it was beautiful. Jeannie and Jay Curry's daughter, Alecia, were getting married. They used to live across the road from us when I was growing up. One day their house burnt to the ground, and they sold the property soon after. I loved that they were my neighbors. Shannon and I used to watch Ashleigh and Alecia when they were little before she had Jaycob. I was able to bring Jaylynn to the wedding, and she was able to play with her friend Olivia from school. Olivia is Jeannie and Jay's adopted daughter. Jeannie is a fantastic mother and foster parent. Jaylynn had a blast attending her first wedding; she was excited to be able to play with other children.

As for me, I sat back and enjoyed the evening. At one point, I couldn't find Jaylynn. Casey told me to go enjoy myself, and he would find her. I was impressed with how he took care of her like she was his own. On top of how he just generally had her best interest at heart, watching them dance together at the wedding was so adorable. It melted my heart and brought a tear to my eyes. We sat with my parents at the wedding, and my mother looked at me as I stared at Casey and Jaylynn on the dance floor.

"Jess, he is one great guy. Please don't ever let him go," said Mom.

I told both her and Dad how happy I was and that I couldn't ever picture my life being anything else than what it was at that very moment.

I thanked God that night for bringing him into my life; for so long, I thought I was going to be a single mother forever. I thought I would not be able to love or trust again; Casey proved me wrong. Not only was my heart open, but I fell in love again. Most importantly, I could trust him.

In the past, I had given up so much in my life for men. He made me realize I don't have to be the only one who sacrificed throughout a relationship. We both felt that we made a good team. My strong character and his understanding of life—together we just *worked*. He could always simplify a situation and make me see different sides; he was good at making me feel better about any problem. He had a gentle touch that would calm me when I was having a rough day. I love that about him. He was the only one that could ever make me feel that I was worthy of anything and everything.

He always used to say don't be scared to ask me for help. I think that he would get a little flustered because he knew I was so used to doing things myself, and I was hesitant to accept the help. It would bother him because I would never ask him for help when I needed it. He would make fun of my stubborn personality and make me laugh as always.

***

The Friday night before Scott and Angie's wedding, I was going to bring up my truck to Casey so he could just come down in the morning to get ready.

"Babe, don't worry about it right now," he sighed. "I am dealing with something right now."

"Ok, is everything alright?"

"Yes, everything is fine. I will see you in the morning, babe, I have to go take care of Webb. Make sure you wear something comfortable and to wear tennis shoes because I am going to take you someplace in the morning."

It cracked me up every time he says tennis shoes because I call them sneakers.

"Ok," I chuckled. "I will see you in the morning, babe."

But little did I know what exactly he was doing. Apparently, he got ahold of Steve and Barb to help him out. He asked Steve to take him to the Falls to set up a place to hide the message in the bottle. Steve had mentioned to Casey previously that it was a great place. That Friday night, he was hiking down the trails to get to the bottom of the Falls with Steve to set up his surprise for me!

I picked him up at the barracks and slid into the passenger's seat because he wanted to drive. Our first stop is Denny's for breakfast.

"Is this the place you wanted to take me?" I asked.

He smiled and didn't say a word.

As persistent as I am, I had to joke around about it. It was great to sit down and enjoy our breakfast together because we never got that many opportunities to be alone.

We finished up breakfast and headed south on I-81 towards my parents' house. Casey decides to get off of Pulaski exit headed towards Altmar on Route 13.

"Where are we going?" I asked for the umpteenth time. "Are we going to Barb and Steve's house?" He knew where they lived, and we hung out there a handful of times.

"Nope, you'll see."

As we approach the Town of Altmar, he decided to take a left turn onto County Route 22, which is the way to Salmon River Falls. I was patiently waiting to see if he was going to take me there. We passed by Falls Road, so I had to interject.

"If your plan was to take me to Salmon River Falls, I hope you know that you passed the road that says Falls Road."

"Shit," he chuckled.

"Do you know where you're going?" I asked.

"Yes," he said firmly.

When we pull up to the Falls, we get out, and he grabs his backpack. "We're going to hike down to the bottom of the Falls," he said calmly.

"After all the years of living in this area, I have never been to the bottom of the Falls," I admitted. "I've heard a lot of people falling, so I guess I'm kinda scared."

"Don't worry, babe," he said softly, "I'll take care of you and help you all the way down."

I felt a little better about the situation, but I was still nervous. As we headed down the trail, I noticed that they did a lot of work on making stairs to make it easier to step down the steep side of the ravine. It was an interesting hike down. He had to grab me a couple of times to lift me down and hold my hand, but he was a complete gentleman and kept me safe. I didn't have to worry about him because he is a strong masculine man who can definitely hold his weight and then some.

We finally reached the bottom of the trail and stopped to take pictures of the Falls. Casey decided he wanted to get closer to them. There was a family down there, and their kids were playing in the water. Casey found this big rock for us to sit on to rest. I got back up because I found a small Gatorade bottle with a piece of paper in it. It reminded me of pirates sending hidden messages.

"Look at this, do you think someone is trying to find their true love?" I asked sarcastically. "I want to open it and see what's on the paper. I'll just make sure I put it back so the person looking for it can find it."

I unscrewed the top and stuck my finger in the bottle to pry the paper out. I opened the paper and started reading it. As I was reading the letter, I realized that it was all about my daughter and me. It talked about how Casey wanted to be with me for the rest of his life and that he loved Jaylynn and me so much that he couldn't picture his life without us in it. He told me that he would devote his life to being the best husband and father that he could possibly be. As he went on to say that he loved me, he decided to pop the question, "Will you marry me?"

As I turned around to look at him, he was down on one knee, with a ring box holding it up to me. As I began to cry with tears of joy, he verbally asked me, "Jess, will you do me the honor and become my wife?"

As tears were rolling down my face, I instantly said, "YES!"

He got up off his knee, and I looked at the ring—I was in shock that it was the same exact ring that he loved at Kay Jewelers. I hugged him so tightly that he could barely even put the ring on my finger. I kissed him and kissed him so much that he grabbed ahold of me and wouldn't let me go. After a minute or so, he put the ring on my finger and told me he had something else for me. He pulled out a bottle of Red Cat wine and popped the cork. Barb had told him that Red Cat was my favorite! He pulled out two red solo cups to celebrate our engagement.

After we sat on the big rock soaking up the view and enjoying nature while we drank our wine, we talked about our future. He expressed that he wanted me to know that I was his forever. We both knew that he was deploying, and we both had questions and concerns about how our relationship would survive. Still, this engagement meant the world to both of us. It was totally unexpected and happened so quickly, but in the same sense, it felt natural. From the day I met Casey, he completely stole my heart, and I knew that he was the man with whom I was to spend the rest of my life.

I was dying to know how he managed to get my ring. How did he pull that off? I asked him how and when he had the time to go get it. He told me that when we went to the mall with Jaylynn and said he was shopping for his mother, it was just an excuse for us to look at rings. He pretended to talk to the salesperson about a gift for his mother, but in reality, he was getting me the perfect ring and needed to keep it a secret. He played it off very well. The best part is that he picked out the ring that he loved just as much as I did. That was precious because he said once I put that ring on, he knew it was the one even before he said anything to me or before I mentioned anything as well. It's funny how we both connected on a deeper level than either could have imagined. I have never felt so complete than I did when he was by my side. The three of us were on our way to becoming a happy family.

We were enjoying our time together and didn't realize that we had to leave and get ready for the wedding. I was curious as to how my parents were going to react. On our way back to my house, I asked Casey how we were going to tell my parents. Casey told me that he wanted to tell my parents personally, so he did.

He sat before them in our living room and told my dad and my mother how he felt about Jaylynn and me. My parents were both shocked and extremely happy. They knew that he was the one for me and that he was going to be a great father to Jaylynn. That was the most important thing to them. They wanted to be certain that Jaylynn had that perfect father figure in her life because that is what she deserved.

My dad shook Casey's hand with a manly pat on the back while my mother kissed him on the cheek and gave Casey a big hug. Of course, the first question out of my father's mouth was, "So, when is the wedding with the open bar?" We all chuckled because if anyone knows my father, he is a complete smart ass. A funny, smart ass! Maybe even a little perverted for an old man!

After the time we took to talk to my mom and dad, it was time to get ready for the wedding. Jaylynn had stayed over at Aunt Shannon's house and played with her girls while we attended the wedding. Casey and I decided that we were not going to say anything or post anything on Facebook because it was my best friend's special day. I didn't want to take away from their moment or be disrespectful to them, but it was hard to hide the big diamond on my finger.

As we were waiting for the wedding to start, I kept looking at Casey, feeling so proud that one day soon I would be his wife. I had butterflies in my stomach that were not going away. I was glowing with happiness. People told me that night that they never saw me so happy in all the years they had known me. I thought to myself, *Is it that noticeable to everyone right now?* But I didn't care what anybody thought. I was extremely happy.

The wedding was beautiful, and Angie was so gorgeous. I was so happy for them. They looked like the perfect couple. After the wedding, we proceeded to walk to Wysockis Manor to be seated. It was an open bar for the first hour. My mom and dad got their drinks and sat at the table. My sister and her husband Jimmer sat with us. There was one seat left for Jodi who had officiated Scott and Angie's wedding.

"Is this seat open?" asked Jodi.

"Yes, it is," my mom grinned. "Come join us!" Jodi seemed so down to earth, and by our conversations, she seems like a great person. She had no idea what she was about to witness with our conversations. We all had a good time at our table because, once again, Dad was being a jokester and started talking about "shrinkage." I can remember Dad said that after being married for so long, it only shrinks. That is how the conversation came about.

Of course, my mom went along with it regarding their sex life, but Shannon and I didn't want to hear about that. Dad did not care; he would continue the perverted conversation. Then Casey joined in, and between them both, all of us at the table were laughing so hard we were crying.

It was hard to go unnoticed. I can remember Keith Lamica coming over and saying that he was going to join our table because it looked like fun. Not only did we laugh, but we also had a great conversation regarding mine and Casey's engagement. Jodi had given Casey her card, so when we decided to get married, she would be more than happy to perform the ceremony.

Mom and Dad were proud to announce to a couple of people that we were getting married. I was starting to think that they were seriously ready to get rid of me. I knew they were just as excited as Casey and me. As the night went on, we were happy that we were a part of their night. It was a great night for everyone. Casey and I decided to leave at the same time as Mom and Dad to make sure they got home alright.

When we got to the house, we all stayed up until midnight, still talking about how the wedding was and our engagement. My mom and dad were asking us when we thought that we were going to get married. We decided to get married when he got back from his deployment, and I would plan the wedding while he was gone. I can remember my mom started to tear up, telling us that she was happy for us and how grateful she was to welcome Casey into our family.

Of course, we all had a couple drinks, so our emotions were running high. As my mom and I were having a moment overcome with emotion, I told my parents I was going to bed because I could not keep my eyes open any longer. So, we said good night and went to bed.

***

I woke up the next morning, thinking it was a dream. I felt something foreign on my ring finger because I am not used to wearing rings on that hand. I looked at my ring and was still in shock that this man staring me in the eyes first thing in the morning, literally asked me to marry him. I can remember the smile he gave me that morning when he woke up.

"I can't wait for you to be my wife," he said gently I feel like I am the luckiest man in the world to have such a beautiful woman and such an amazing little girl who is my daughter."

"I can't wait for you to be my husband and start our new adventure as a family. I want it more than anything!"

I truly loved every moment I got to spend with him. He has the biggest heart and loved how he expressed his feelings. I hated the fact that I had to bring him back to the barracks. I knew that I would have to drive him back up to Fort Drum at some point that day and wanted to soak him up for as long as I could. I had an idea. Maybe, since we were engaged now, he could possibly stay longer if I were to give him the keys to my Chevy Trailblazer. He could drive himself back so I wouldn't have to. He agreed and was able to stay longer.

I still had my Volkswagen Jetta to drive, so it made it easier for him to come down and see us during the week. It was extremely hard for him to come down that far to see us. I asked my mom if she could watch Jaylynn one night a week so I could go up there to see him. Well, needless to say, my mom and I butted heads.

I can remember I called Casey one night crying because I couldn't deal with it anymore. I guess once you have had enough, you break down. Don't get me wrong, I love my mom, but she is not the easiest person to live with. But I sold my house and moved in with them so I could build a house next to my parents. My dad cleared the property next to their house, and my parents were going to deed me an acre of land so Jaylynn and I could build a little house next to them. I was close with my parents, and Jaylynn was even closer to them.

Jaylynn loved to go back in the woods with my dad to check the deer cameras and ride the trails with the four-wheeler. Personally, I couldn't live with my mother because we have separate ways on how we like things. I couldn't deal with the negative lifestyle that she lives. She would get really moody and angry when I didn't do something that she wanted me to do but never asked for me to do it. I think that she expected me to read minds and just know what she wanted me to do around the house.

I was never home. I was working full time, and I didn't have all the time in the world at night to stay home and take care of things. I had responsibilities too. I just didn't know what I could do to make her happy at that point. She never goes anywhere or enjoys hardly anything. Because she never leaves the house, when she does, she becomes anxious.

Casey had three weeks before he was set to deploy, and he suggested that we get married in front of the justice of the peace before he left.

"I was already thinking about it because if we're not married, the military won't give you any information about me while I'm gone. My sergeant told me that it would be near impossible to get married and set us up with everything within two weeks because

I'm going to be busy. Just bear with your mom at your parents' house until I get back, or we can find you an apartment, and I'll pay for it in the meantime."

I agreed to find an apartment because I needed some personal space away from my mother. He put me on his USAA account to manage his funds, and I would have a deposit on an apartment. He calmed me down and told me that it will get better. He kept reminding me that I was—and still am—a strong independent woman.

"You got this, babe," he said. I knew that our marriage was going to be a lasting relationship.

He called, telling me that he had bad news and good news.

"Which one would you like to hear first?" he asked.

"I personally always go with the bad news first, so the good news can brighten up the day a little."

"Okay, well, the bad news is that I'm going to be really busy for the next couple of days. You'll have to bear with me."

"Okay," I frowned. I hated not being able to spend every single moment I could with him before he left.

"The good news is that we're going to get married before I leave."

I didn't think I would ever hear those words come out of his mouth. He talked to one of his guys and said that it could be done before he left. It would be a lot of paperwork for his commanding officers to complete the process, but he didn't care. All he cared about was getting Jaylynn and I into a house on post, so he could return to his girls and our new home.

He told me all the benefits that we would have by getting married before he left, including insurance for Jaylynn and me, along with an increase of pay for us and our very own home. I agreed with him, and I was completely happy with the decision that he made to take care of us. I was madly in love with him because he was willing to take good care of us even while he was deployed. I couldn't wait to be Mrs. Brewer.

We made several attempts to reach Jodi so that she could marry us. We couldn't get ahold of her, but he told me to keep trying. There was so much that needed to be arranged and taken care of prior to my becoming Mrs. Brewer.

The following day, we had to go get our marriage license. When I finally spoke to Jodi, she said that we would have to wait 48 hours after getting our marriage license before she could marry us. It was the law. I called Casey on my lunch break and told him the situation. He told me that he was able to come down that afternoon so we can get the marriage license. I left work early, met Casey at Ezze Truck Stop, and we drove to Oswego, New York, to the County Clerk's Office. Once we got there, we paid for our marriage license and got the paperwork for Jodi.

Jodi also advised us that we both had to have a witness. Casey told me that his friend, Alex Arnone, would be his witness. I had called my sister, but she said she had to work. So, I called Barb and asked her. She was so ecstatic to be a part of my special moment.

Casey and I discussed that since he proposed to me at the bottom of the Salmon River Falls, it would be perfect to get married on top of those same Falls. I loved his idea because he made the proposal so special for me. I couldn't have agreed more to saying I do to him in that very spot.

Casey and I discussed our options for wedding bands, and he wanted silver wedding bands for both of us. He actually picked out sterling silver wedding bands at Walmart. I didn't care that they were cheap bands; I was just happy he made an effort and picked them out himself. I was so proud of him. He told me that someday we would get better wedding bands, but I treasured the one he had purchased for me that day. I didn't need a new one. I wanted him to know and show him that I didn't care about material things, nor did I expect expensive things. He wanted me to have nice things because he knew all the sacrifices I had made in my life and thought that I deserved it all. He was definitely a blessing.

We made arrangements with Jodi to get married at Salmon River Falls on Wednesday, October 23, 2013. I was both nauseous and nervous that morning at work. After all, this was a *huge* step in my life. Casey and I both wanted Jaylynn to be there when we got married, so I left work early and went to pick Jaylynn up from school.

We met Casey, Arnone, and Barb at the Falls. Jodi arrived shortly after. When she got there, everything got so surreal. It was cold, windy, and drizzling rain. We brought an umbrella because who knew if it was going to start pouring down. We got out of our vehicles and walked down the trail to the steps that take you to the top of the Falls. I looked at Casey like nothing else mattered at all. I was going to spend the rest of my life with this man and Jaylynn. All I could think about was how proud I was to be a part of his life.

As we picked out our spot on the Falls to say our vows, we could feel the sprinkling of mist. It was starting to rain as well. Jodi said kind and loving words regarding our life together. Casey said his vows first, and when it came time to say mine, I was shivering because of the cold damp mist in the air. I didn't care, though.

I looked in Casey's eyes and said, "I do. In the rain and in the cold, I do, I do." It became an instant memory for us because it made everyone laugh.

Jodi said some inspirational words of wisdom for our marriage, and it was time for the kiss. The look in his eyes was all about me and only me. I felt like I was the only person in Casey's universe. I thought my heart was going to explode. The first kiss as husband and wife was the most memorable. With Casey holding the umbrella as I held his frozen hand and kissed his icy cold lips, I didn't want the moment to end. He held me close as he wrapped his arms around me.

I needed his warmth for a minute, but I knew that Casey and Arnone had to get back up to Fort Drum. Thank God Barb was there because she took pictures during the wedding. Jodi had to have us sign our marriage paperwork along with Arnone and Barb as our witnesses. Jodi let us take the marriage license with our sworn statements and witnesses to Oswego to get our certified marriage certificate started.

We also had to go pick up my new car at Burritt Motors. I bought a silver 2013 Chevrolet Malibu with leather seats. I loved that car until I realized that there was a water leak in the rear trunk area. Once we went to the County Clerk office and submitted the paperwork for our marriage and picked up our car, it was time for Casey and Arnone to leave. Casey said his goodbyes to me at my parent's house.

"Goodbye, Mrs. Brewer," he said as he looked me in my eyes.

"Goodbye, Mr. Brewer."

For me to hear him say my new name was so heart-warming. I loved it. I was sad that we couldn't spend our first night being married together. He assured me that we would have many years to be in each other's arms.

***

I hadn't been talking to my mother because we had been fighting. Dad wanted me to take the camera to have pictures. I didn't invite my parents or give them a lot of information, but they knew what was happening. I knew that my parents left to take my grandparents to see Grandpa's sister, Aunt Evie, who was in a nursing home. When they got back, Dad saw the pictures. They were sad that they missed it. Funny thing is that Casey's parents didn't even know. He was going to tell them that weekend.

The weekend had come, and I went to pick up Casey. As we were headed back to my parent's house, Casey called his parents to let them know that we had gotten married. I know his father was in shock and didn't want to talk much. His mom, on the other hand, was the one who talked to both of us. I realized that it was a shock and a lot to take in, especially since they have never met me at all. I loved their son with everything I had, but I could see it was difficult for them.

Casey started to talk to me about his father and his upbringing. He continued to tell me that his father is not a very sociable person. I wanted them to say congratulations, but he was silent. I expected the conversation to be more pleasant than it was. Considering that his parents had never met me, how was it supposed to go? I guess I was living in a fantasy expecting their immediate approval. They were the only ones that may have been a little disappointed in us.

My father was kind of disappointed because I was his last daughter to get married. He was sad that he didn't have the chance to walk me down the aisle. Both of my parents never thought that I would ever get married, so they were just happy for us. The look on my dad's face when he expressed his disappointment about not being able to walk me down the aisle hurt my heart. So, Casey and I decided to have a family wedding to allow Dad to give me away. Also, we wanted to share our special moments with everyone.

Once again, we were sitting in my parent's living room discussing our future wedding. Casey said that we had to pick a date; I would have nine months to plan a perfect day for us. We also decided that we would ask Barb and Steve to stand up for us. They happily agreed to do so. My sister was a given.

I didn't have to ask her—she was my sister. When I told her that I was already married, that's when I asked her to be my matron of honor. She, too, had her reservations because we weren't together that long, but she was happy for me regardless. She also knew that I was such a hard person to please because I was so picky. I had to be because of Jaylynn. I wanted the best for her too, and I found it in Casey.

We had a week and a half before Casey was to be deployed. He went through housing and got us our first house on base. I was so thrilled!! Looking back now, that place was so tiny. It was a two-bedroom duplex with one and a half bathrooms. I was not thrilled about the driving every day from Fort Drum to Brewerton, which is located in the Town of Cicero, for work. I was, however, ecstatic that we had our very first home together.

I can remember that Casey asked like 5 or 6 guys to help me move out of my parents' house. It was kind of crazy that day. My mother was being rude to the guys that came to help, but I was just thankful to get out of there. I had gotten rid of a lot of my belongings prior, so I didn't have much furniture. I only had my daughter's bed, my bed, and dressers.

I did keep all my kitchen utensils, pots, and pans. Casey rented a U-Haul truck, so I filled garbage bags with my clothing and loaded all the boxes with the rest of my belongings. I said goodbye to my mother, but she didn't say one word to me. I was to the point now that I would never look back. I was happy, and that is all that mattered.

As I was unpacking, the guys sat in fold-out chairs in the living room and played video games. It was great. Jaylynn dressed everyone up in leftover black plastic bags like they needed a redneck raincoat. It was funny to see her top their heads with ribbons and bows.

Casey's friends Arnone and Heath were always at our house before they left for deployment. I took the time to make them home-cooked meals a few times because I knew they wouldn't get a decent meal over there. We got the house set up as much as Casey and I could. I knew the dreaded day was coming that he was going to leave. My heart was aching, but I knew we would be ok.

***

When the day finally came, we both got up at 4 a.m. I had to get up and make that long ass ride to work, and he had to get ready to leave.

The first thing he says to me in the morning is, "Good morning, Beautiful."

We both went downstairs to make coffee. I was just looking at him like *Man, I am going to miss him.*

"What?" he asks, feeling my stares.

"I don't know how I am going to do this without you!" I felt the tears started to form.

"Baby, the one thing that I fell in love with you the most was that you're so strong and independent. I knew that when I would leave, I wouldn't have to worry about you because you're such an amazing woman."

That did it. I started crying so hard and hugged him as tight as I could.

"Baby, it's not like I am not coming back. Don't worry, once I get back, we will have our family wedding! We can finally start on our family!"

"Yes," I nodded. "I love you, Baby!"

"Baby, I love you more!" I still felt like my heart was being ripped out of my chest. My mind could not grasp what was about to happen. I had to pull myself together.

Once I finished my coffee, it was time for me to get in the shower. When I turned on the water, I couldn't control it anymore. Tears flooded my face, and I started whimpering in agony. I couldn't believe that my soulmate was about to leave me. Casey heard me bawling in the bathroom, and he came in to comfort me.

"Baby, don't cry," he said soothingly. "I don't want this to be the last memory of my wife before I leave."

"I'm sorry," I sniffled, "I just can't help it. I love you, and I don't want you to go."

It was so hard for me to understand this life I was about to live. I had no clue what I had gotten myself into. I thought I was a soldier's wife, living the American Dream with my husband and starting a family. I had a lot to learn, aside from just being his wife. *This is when my life changed forever.*

***

I didn't hear from him for at least two weeks after he left. It drove me nuts not knowing if he made it or not or if he was safe. It wasn't even one week after he had left that I got a knock at the door at 3 a.m. The doorbell was ringing like crazy. I looked through the peephole and saw four military police officers standing outside. I opened the door immediately.

"Oh, God," I gasped. "Is everything okay? Is Casey okay?"

"Can we have your name please, ma'am?" asked the officer in the middle.

"Jessica Brewer."

The officers looked at each other with confusion. "Hold on just a second," said the same cop as he walked back to their car.

"What is going on here?" I demanded, but the other cops weren't paying me any attention. I was so scared that something had happened to Casey. The worst fear of all was thinking the plane went down or something.

A few minutes later, the officer came back from the car. "Sorry to disturb you at this hour, but we had a call for domestic violence. This is the wrong house."

"Are you fucking kidding me?" I said annoyed. I told them how I felt about them coming to my house at 3 a.m. when my husband was deployed. I thought they were going to put me in handcuffs because I was so angry. I cussed them out and stressed the fact that they had me extremely worried. I eventually calmed down as they expressed their sincerest apologies. Needless to say, I couldn't go back to sleep after that because my nerves were too worked up.

I can remember the first time Casey called me when he was out of the country. I was at work, so I left my desk and went into the conference room to talk to him. I told him what had happened to me with the Military Police knocking at our door. He just busted out laughing, but I didn't think it was funny. He told me that if someone were going to tell me something, it wouldn't be the Military Police.

***

Casey told me to start planning the family wedding, which kept me busy most of the time. I would get up at 5 a.m. and leave at 6:00 a.m. to be at work by 8 a.m. If it was snowing out, which happened quite frequently, I would get up at 4 a.m. and leave by 5:30 a.m. It was an awful drive when it was snowing, especially coming home in a blizzard at nighttime.

Upstate New York got the worst weather in the winter. We would get heavy amounts of snow coming off of Lake Ontario. It would be feet on top of feet of snow, and I would travel straight through it. This weather caused many road closures. Many times, I would have to take detours because there would be multiple car accidents.

I can remember Casey respectfully telling me to put in my two-week notice. At this point, I had to because I was endangering not only my life but my daughter's life making this commute. It was a difficult decision because I loved my job and the people I worked for. I couldn't keep making the drive when I was living in a different county.

I recall that one night I was on my way home, and we were getting freezing rain and sleet. Out of nowhere, a tractor-trailer almost ran us off the road, and I was a hot mess driving home. As we got closer to home and I turned on Baldwin Circle, my car literally slid down the hill. I could not stop until I hit a snowbank. That was the deal-breaker. I knew that I had to resign.

***

As time went on with me being home by myself, I had a lot of time to realize how much I missed my husband. I fantasized about our life together. Not only was I planning the wedding while he was gone, but I began researching opportunities to work from home. I also performed house closings. It was fun, and I loved it. So, I set a new goal for myself to get my business off the ground, and I did.

I told Casey about my business that I was working on, and I needed to go get a new computer and a business printer. He fully supported me on any decision that I made, and I loved that about him. I did research on getting a laptop and printer that works faster than the one I had. It would literally take an hour and a half to print 250 pages for a job where other printers would take minutes to do the same thing. I had to take a test and get my background check before anyone would hire me. After I completed those tasks, I was able to get everything I needed to proceed to work.

My business took off. I couldn't believe the work that I was able to get. Needless to say, between work and planning our family wedding, I was extremely busy.

***

Casey and I had to discuss who was going to be in our wedding party, and we finally made a decision on who would stand up for us. Once we finally decided on who we wanted, I went about looking for dresses. I wanted to have something elegant but also something everyone could afford. The girls found a dress that was flowy and sleeveless. I absolutely fell in love with it. It was a dress that everyone liked, which was great because you usually always have that *one* person that doesn't like something.

Since the girls were out of the way, I started the process of finding a dress for myself. I picked out three wedding gowns to try on. I knew I wanted my dress to be sleeveless, and I tried on two of the gowns and found that they were not what I wanted. Once I tried on my last dress, it felt amazing. The dress was beautiful and had different layers of sheer elegant material. The corset backing was tricky but totally worth it. As soon as I tried it on, I knew that was the one and didn't need to look any further.

My wedding photographer, Gena, made sure that my dress was tied properly and fit perfectly. Gena is an amazing, caring person. I knew Gena from when we worked together at Cedar Pines. Her sister Val worked there as well. Val and I had a lot of fun together, especially at my 21st birthday party when my parents were out of town.

Kim, the owner of Cedar Pines, gave me a bottle of Apple Pucker for my birthday. Val and I left work to head to my house, and I pretty much threw a party. My parents warned me not to have any parties at the house, but I just had to have one anyway. Who listens to their parents when they are out of town? Mom and Dad, if you're reading this, I am so sorry that your vodka bottle was filled with water. I was going to replace it, but I forgot. I love you!

Val and I didn't have an uncontrollable party. We had a couple drinks and hopped into my dad's plow truck and plowed the driveway before all my friends showed up. It was a couple people... well, okay, maybe 20 people showed up. It was a fun night.

We girls have a lot of memories of Cedar Pines. I met my buddy Caza there. He and I partied a lot together. I knew if I needed anything, he would be right there to help me. I used to love hearing about all of his women, and I would bust on him all the time to stay away from the crazies. He always came into the bar to hang with us girls. Heather, Jessica, Val, Gena, Jessica, Crystal, and I were famous at the restaurant, and people loved to see us each and every week.

***

Long story short, Gena moved, and we reunited with her, taking modeling pictures for me. Right before Casey and I met, she encouraged me to get back on track to put together my portfolio. I had a company email me regarding my pictures that were taken when I was 18 years old. They asked me if I would be interested in doing freelance work. Of course, I accepted and was excited. I had to get my portfolio together and send it to them so I could possibly do some modeling on the side and earn extra money. Gena helped me by setting up a photoshoot.

After a month or so, we decided to go to New York City and shoot some photos there. While we were down there, I was going to drop off my portfolio to other companies, but I didn't have time. We had a lot of fun, plus I was able to see my cousin Dan.

After the New York City trip, I met Casey, and he was everything that I needed in life. I forgot about who I wanted to be and who I really was at that time. What I wanted in life was to get married and add to our family. Give my daughter her dream of having a sibling.

***

I must say, trying on the wedding dress for the first time made me think of how much I loved that man and how I am going to proclaim my love for him in front of my whole family and all my friends. Nobody and I mean *nobody* thought I would ever get married.

Even though many of my years consisted of being single, some women despised me. Barb always told me that women were jealous of me. Most saw me as a threat back then, like I was going to take their man from them or something. Jealously causes a lot of people to do evil in this world. My best friend Barb and I would always sit there and talk about how people are just so jealous at times and that those people shouldn't be a part of our world if they have issues like that.

Once everyone found out that I was getting married, it seemed like it was a relief for not only myself for being hated but, most importantly, the others for not having to worry about their husbands. I was never a cheater or a liar. It's not who I am. Truthful and straight forward is how I rolled in life. My daughter taught me that even more so when she was born.

As situations arose in my life, I began to change; I became a bitch. I was sick of getting stepped on and used like a doormat. At a certain time in my life, people would look at me as a girl that was not to be messed with. I am still not to be messed with, but my personality has relaxed. There is always a place and a time for everything. I care deeply about how I am perceived by others. Our family's image as a dedicated, loving family is all I could ever ask for.

***

Preparing for my wedding was my dream since I was a little girl. I think most little girls dream about being Sleeping Beauty or Cinderella, and that is exactly how I felt. I was about to marry the man of my dreams, my Prince Charming. As thrilled as I was about marrying Casey and pledging our love in front of our family and friends, in the back of my mind, I still was afraid. My husband was deployed and didn't know when he was coming home.

With all the excitement around planning the wedding and establishing my business, my old love was around the corner. It was softball season! It was my second year with Driveway Inn, and I was ecstatic for the season to start the first week in May. Sydney and I would take trips down to my hometown and practice with the girls before the season began. Sydney was one of my close friends at Fort Drum.

We would wait until my daughter got off the bus, then head down to scrimmage with another team. Other times, we would just hit some balls. It was great too, because Jaylynn loved going to all my games; she was like the team mascot. She would always go wherever I would go. Once in a while, she would stay with my mom and dad but not very often because they always went to my games too.

I really wish that I would have gotten to play with my sister. She and I played together and had our own team, Endzone, for many years. It got to be too much for her due to the kids' busy schedules. I continued to play. It was the one night a week to which I absolutely looked forward to, and it was so much fun. I got to play with my friends Skittles, Erika, Sydney, Jenn, and all the other amazing girls on the team. I always wanted Casey to watch me play if he got out of work early enough.

***

Casey got back from deployment because of an injury. When I heard that he blew out his knee during an attack, I was so scared. I hadn't heard anything from him for weeks. I knew he was on a mission. I wasn't even contacted by the FRG or Commander regarding this incident, which was upsetting.

I found out when Casey messaged me through Facebook Messenger.

```
Hey Jess has anyone had contacted you?
                                          No. Why?
Are you home?
                         Not yet. Give me a few minutes.
                         Just went grocery shopping.
Okay see you in a bit.
```

Once I logged onto Skype, I messaged him telling him I was ready. As soon as his face pops up, I am smiling from ear to ear.

"Babe has anyone contacted you?" he asked.

"No, why? Was someone supposed to call me?"

"Do you want the good news first or the bad news first?"

"Give me the bad news first! What happened, babe?"

"Well, something happened, and there was an attack... and I got injured. But the good news is that I am ok."

"Oh my God, baby, what happened?"

"The details don't matter. I don't want to worry you."

"Ok."

"Baby, as far as I know right now, I will be headed to Germany for surgery."

"Well, I don't have my passport to come to be with you."

"It's ok babe, I will be home before you know it."

I was nervous because I didn't have my passport to travel there to be by his side. Things kept changing after that. We were told that after the surgery, they were also going to send him to rehab in Virginia. At that time, he didn't know when he was going to be home. The only thing the medics gave him for the pain was Tylenol and Motrin. I felt so helpless knowing that he didn't have any relief.

A week or more goes by, and we Skype again. This time, he tells me that he will be coming home for surgery and recovering at home. I couldn't be happier to hear those words. He also said that it was going to take him a couple weeks to get home. It was all the different stops they had to make to refuel and board another plane. They were only allowed to follow a certain route. It was great that he was coming home, but I was so worried about him.

I still did not know exactly what happened the day he was injured. He always told me that he didn't want me to worry and that if it was important, then he would tell me. I felt like I had to know because I was his wife. If I knew what he was going through, then I would be able to understand and be there for him emotionally.

There was no handbook on deployments and how to support your spouse mentally and emotionally. I wanted to be that support for my husband. For the first time, I realized that there was more to this military life than I thought.

***

The two weeks it took for him to arrive felt like forever. He would try to connect to the internet to update me on his status of where he was and the route they were taking to get to their next location. He got stuck in Germany for a week for some reason that is still unbeknownst to me to this day. I respected him for not telling me; he knew that I was on pins and needles waiting for his return.

He finally told me that he was boarding a plane in the middle of the night with one line: "Baby, I am boarding the plane now, I will message you when I land." When I wake and see the message, my mind started racing. Where was he going? When would he land, and how long would it be before he arrived home to me? I always kept my ringer on high. It literally was driving me crazy! Every time my phone would ring, I grabbed it in hopes that it would be him with an update.

By the time he had contacted me, it was my day and his night because of the time difference. He was completely exhausted and in extreme pain. One doctor did give him some medication to take the edge off when he was in Germany just to get him home.

I was thankful someone did because Tylenol and Motrin can only do so much with an injury like that. I felt helpless, and I wanted to do something so bad. It was a relief to know that his next stop was going to be in the United States and not a foreign country.

Knowing that he was getting closer to home, my daughter and I went to Walmart to pick out a poster board to make a welcome home sign for his arrival. She was so excited to welcome him home with her artwork. She told me one night that she couldn't wait to have him tuck her into bed. It was a touching moment for me because she wanted him to do what fathers do with their children.

She picked out a tie-dyed poster board that she absolutely loved and designed herself. I talked to Casey when he arrived in the United States, and he was informed that they would fly him directly to Fort Drum. Once again, things changed. He was flying home on Delta Airlines to Hancock Airport in Syracuse.

I told my mom and dad that we would be meeting him at Hancock Air Base to welcome him home. My sister was able to make it there as well. I had to pull Jaylynn from school to meet at my parents' house. I was nervous because I was seeing him for the first time in months, but I was excited to start our life together, living together and expanding our family.

When we arrived at the airport, I was lost. I didn't know which way to go or where to park. Everything was so foreign to me. Once we parked and found our way in, we asked an attendant where the Delta plane would be landing and deboarding passengers. As we were waiting for him to come through the gate to surprise him, Jaylynn had her sign ready to go. My mom even had a camera ready to capture the entire moment.

As we start to see him walking up to the glass doors with crutches, Jaylynn stepped out to welcome her dad home. Seeing him made me feel so emotional that I felt like I had to rush to him and show just how much I missed him. After holding each other for what seemed like forever, I let him go so he could pick Jaylynn up to hug his sweet baby girl. It was such a touching moment. All of us were crying happy tears, even Casey. Jaylynn looked up to Casey so much, and

Casey adored Jaylynn as though she was his own. It felt like our hearts were united as one.

Once we got home, Casey went straight to the shower. Trust me when I say this—his clothes smelled so bad that they could stand up by themselves. All he wanted to do was go home and bathe. He also had one more thing on his mind, and that was me.

The house looked a little different from that last time he saw it. One thing that jumped out and grabbed Casey's attention was that his army boots never left his side of the bed. They were exactly where he left them the day he deployed. We no longer had folding chairs in the living room anymore; we actually had furniture to relax and sit on. One welcome home present that my parents and I bought for him was the new Xbox One. He was happy to see that he got what he wanted. He loves his video games, but they were a nuisance to our marriage. Once he started playing on that thing, he would not come to bed at a decent hour. He would stay up all night and sleep during the day.

With that being said, marrying someone that you hardly know and finding out your differences was challenging for both of us. The best part was understanding how the other felt and working through the challenges. Communication was big for us. I had no problem expressing my concerns and trying to work through things. Sometimes, he didn't think things through before he did them. So, he definitely understood why I felt the way I did. We only lived together for a day before he was deployed, and now that he was home, there was a lot more to learn about each other.

He also had to learn to be a father. The most important thing that both of us had in common is the love we had for one another and Jaylynn. We might not have agreed with each other about everything, but we were both dedicated to working together through all our obstacles. I can definitely say it was a challenge for me, not so much him because he would go with the flow, but me, on the other hand, I was so set in my ways.

***

When he came home from his deployment, I would catch myself looking at him while he was in pain. I would say to myself that I am his wife, and my sense of motherhood kicked in. If I am being honest here, I really didn't know how to be a wife. It was hard to adjust to living with him. I understand the concept of being a wife, but it was much more than just being a wife and taking care of him. It was an overwhelming feeling of belonging, and this was the life I was supposed to live. It wasn't just about Jaylynn and me anymore doing whatever I wanted to do. As a result, I now know what my family has to stand for.

To be seriously honest, I feel that many people live in a bubble. I believe that civilians had no idea about the day to day challenges the soldiers endure to protect our country. I understand that people may have a general concept of our military, but they could never put themselves in the shoes of a soldier for one day. They don't know what it's like sleeping outside on the ground with only grass to comfort them. They can't comprehend living on nothing but an MRE, which is food in a bag. I guess reality smacked me in the face hard.

When Casey and I would talk about the Afghans and their way of living, I was shocked. He told me that women were only used to produce children and that men would have sex with other men and even children at the age of 8. Some would even abuse animals for their self-pleasure. They would urinate and shit in the streets, literally anywhere they wanted. They lived in complete filth for months on end.

For him to see that up close, along with fighting for our country, I don't think anyone in their right mind would feel normal afterward. As we were discussing their culture, I realized that Casey had to live in filth too. I felt so bad for my husband to have to had spent 9 months away from his family to live in unimaginable conditions and witness behavior that was so different than the one to which he was accustomed.

After he got hurt during this deployment, I asked him if it was worth the money and his life to stay in the army.

"I don't get paid enough to do this job," he admitted, "But I love to serve my country. It's all that I know how to do to support my family. That is what matters."

When I had mentioned earlier about living in a bubble, that is exactly how I lived my entire life before I met him. I was focused on raising Jaylynn and getting up every morning to make money to support us. I would watch the news with my parents and see news broadcasts on a daily basis, but I never sat down and thought to myself that someone's mother, daughter, father, or son would lose their life to protect us.

Furthermore, I never considered what those families must feel during tough times. Never in a million years did I think that my life and perspective would change. I felt helpless and knew that I couldn't control anything. You have to learn that these deployments can have a mental impact on your husband. It's frightening to see him walk out that door in the morning and know something could happen.

***

When Casey was still walking around on crutches, we had to rush Jaylynn to the doctors for an injury. She hurt herself in Tehonica's Taekwondo class. She was breaking boards and told me that her foot hurt, and it wasn't going away. I took her to the doctor, and sure enough, she had a stress fracture in her foot so she couldn't go to class for a while. The orthopedist put her in a boot cast for 6 weeks, and she had to use crutches. Now, *two* people in the house were on crutches. I was thankful that Casey was home and that she had only a stress fracture and not multiple broken bones.

As the days went on before Casey's knee surgery, I realized that I found myself and my purpose in life. When Casey and I talked about our future and expanding our family, I knew that this was going to be the biggest adventure yet. I had been waiting for it all my life. The day Casey was getting prepped for surgery, I was overcome with emotion. I knew that I could never live without him.

He was my hero because he saved me. He saved me because I was not in a happy place. I was making bad choices and living the single life with no purpose for myself besides Jaylynn. I wanted to feel loved and appreciated, but I didn't know if I would ever be able to get there. I found out how that felt because Casey made me feel important to him. I remember thanking God for bringing Casey to me and Jaylynn. Because without Casey's love and encouragement, who knows where I would have been. Casey gave me our family, and I could not be more thankful.

I always wanted to have another baby. I was thrilled to have the opportunity to share a special moment like this with him and be the loving, devoted wife he deserves. When I mean only him, I mean there is no other place I'd rather be than wrapped up in his arms, knowing that he is my protector.

I would not have to worry about a thing for the rest of my life because I had him by my side as my life partner. I felt that I had to be even stronger than I was when we originally met because when he left on his first deployment, it was just Jaylynn and me. Now that we are a family, it wasn't just us; I had to take care of him too. I knew that he needed me just as much as I needed him.

In June, Casey was finally scheduled for surgery. It wasn't until after we specified that we wanted to see an off-post doctor that things began to move a lot quicker. That is when Casey saw Dr. Greenky. He scheduled his surgery right away. Dr. Greenky said the surgery was only supposed to be an hour to an hour and a half, but I was in the waiting room for over 3. As you probably guessed, I was getting nervous that something had happened.

I walked up to the nurse's desk and asked, "Do you know how my husband is doing?"

"What is your husband's name?" asked the nurse.

"Casey Brewer."

A moment had passed as she was trying to look him up. "Ma'am, we don't have a patient by that name."

I am looking at the nurse with my eyes bugged out of my head. "Ma'am, I am not trying to be rude right now, but my husband is back there getting surgery on his knee! I would appreciate it if one of you ladies would actually get up and go check on your patient which is my husband. By the way, maybe you should really focus on your patients that walk in here and get surgeries performed."

I couldn't believe nobody even knew his name. I am not going to lie, I kind of went ballistic for a hot minute. I was speechless because this was supposed to be a very reputable place. I must say that I wasn't impressed based on my interaction at the nurse's station.

As the nurse came over to me as I was trying to cool my jets down, she said, "Ma'am, he is in recovery if you want to go back."

"Absolutely. I need to get my husband out of here before he actually loses a limb."

The nurse laughed, and I glared at her. "Do you think I am joking? You didn't even know he was here!" I stormed off. I wasn't a fan at all of this place, but I do love the doctor that did his surgery.

When the nurse came out of the operating room to get me and tell me that he was in recovery, I was able to finally relax. That was the best news that I heard all morning. I also expressed my concerns and dissatisfaction with the front desk not knowing their patients.

As I walked into his recovery room, he was sound asleep from the anesthesia. Gently, I rubbed his head and picked up his hand, outlining his knuckles with my fingertips. Just being by his side and knowing how much he needed me made me feel that I was the lucky one in this relationship.

***

After I got him home and he started to recover, we were talking about how fast the wedding was approaching and how we both wanted to start trying to have a baby of our own. We said that we wanted to get pregnant right after the wedding because who knows when he would have to deploy again. I was perfectly fine with trying. Honestly, I don't think either of us would have objected to the idea. I was having issues, and I had to go see a specialist to talk about fertilization.

At my first exam, they found a spot by my fallopian tube that may have been uterine cancer. They told Casey and I that this spot had closed up my tube and was the source of my pain and discomfort. The doctor continued to advise us that the spot had to be removed before we started in vitro. He also wanted to take samples from my uterus.

We scheduled the procedure, and the doctor told Casey that he could be in the room with me the whole time. It was awkward because I had a scope and video camera up my vagina and two men staring at me. You literally saw the procedure on a TV screen above my head. Talk about having an anxiety attack. Casey didn't like the fact that I kept bleeding during the procedure.

After calling in the nurse to cauterize the spot, the doctor told us that I would be bleeding for a couple days or so. "If you bleed for more than a week, just let him know," he said as he washed his hands. "In the meantime, I'll call you regarding the results as soon as I get them in."

It was a painful procedure. It felt like someone was constantly stabbing me with a knife in the vagina. The piercing cramps were so intense that I couldn't be on my feet at all. I had a hard time walking up the stairs to use our bathroom. Since they had to cauterize the bleeding, all I could smell is burnt flesh of my insides. I was still bleeding, but I was doing everything the doctor ordered me to do. I think that both of us knew it was going to be a long process. I was concerned whether or not I could ever have another baby. That was the one thing that I wanted to give both Casey and Jaylynn—a baby to add to our little family.

I was so discouraged, but Casey always had a bright side to every situation we encountered. He is just so calming. We ended up getting the results back; I did have pre-cancerous cells, which is minor dysplasia. The doctor assured me that it was nothing severe and should not prevent me from getting pregnant. If after 3 months, we couldn't get pregnant, we were supposed to go back and discuss a treatment plan. At this point, I told Casey if it was meant to be then it was meant to be. I wasn't going to worry about it. We had enough going on with the wedding and his recovery. I thought that was enough to handle at that point.

I took my frustrations out by playing softball. One night, we were playing Ma Bakers. Half of my old team from End Zone was on that team. It was kind of a rivalry but not really. There were some girls on the team that I didn't care for, and they never cared for me either. All I cared about is winning. That didn't happen, unfortunately. I can remember me being up to bat, and I hit the ball and was running to first base when I accidentally hyperextended my leg. I never felt so much pain. That night is a blur.

The next day, I felt like a dump truck ran over my head and my leg. I went to the doctor, and he sent me for an MRI. Two days later, the doctor had called and told me that I had fractured my tibia. She told me absolutely no walking on it because it was delicate, and there was a chance it could split down to my ankle. I was petrified because our wedding was around the corner and I was walking on it. She sent me to go get X-rays of my tibia so I can go to an orthopedist later that week.

A few days after, Casey took me to the orthopedist.

"Well," said the doctor, "You cracked the top of the tibia which could be dangerous if you don't stay off your leg."

"That is what my doctor said that it could split down to my ankle," I said patiently.

"Yes, and that is why I need to cast you from the hip down to your foot."

I looked at Casey like the doctor *had* to be joking, right? Casey looked at me like, *Oh, hell no!*

"Hey, Doc," said Casey, "We are getting married in 6 weeks and if you decide to cast my wife right now before our family wedding, I can guarantee you that she will be in my father-in-law's garage hacksawing the cast off!"

The doctor looked at Casey and then looked at me as I was nodding my head yes with a shitty-ass grin on my face. Casey knew me well, and he was right, I would be sawing it off. The doctors chuckled and said, "Well. we have only one other option, but you really have to stay off your leg!"

Casey and I definitely wanted to hear this other solution. "We can put you in a stabilizer cast, which is adjustable, but you have to keep it locked at all times."

"Even Better!" I shouted. We agreed to it. Even though it was a pain in the ass to deal with, it was better than the first option.

***

After some weeks go by and I am putting the final touches on our wedding, I felt like I was turning into a bridezilla. I was starting to feel nauseous, and I thought I was having wedding jitters. I didn't tell Casey that I was going to take a pregnancy test because I didn't want to get his hopes up again. I decided to take it before I got in the shower. As I was showering, I just felt awful. The hot water made me even more nauseous, so I tried to hurry up and get out. As I was getting out, I happened to look at the test, and it said pregnant! I literally screamed for Casey.

Casey came bolting up the stairs yelling to see if I was ok. He thought that I had fallen in the shower due to my broken tibia. He found out quickly as he whipped the bathroom door open to find me standing there with my mouth open.

"Baby look!" I screamed. The excitement on his face after he read the test was priceless. He instantly grabbed me to hug me tightly, not knowing his strength was cutting my airway off in my throat. We both were overjoyed with the news.

"My heart was pounding so hard that I felt it in my toes," said Casey between kisses. "I thought you fell down or something, so I flew up the stairs."

"Baby, we are pregnant!!" I couldn't stop smiling.

"Babe, this is the best gift you could have ever given me right now."

He helped me get dressed, and it finally hit us that not only did I have a broken tibia, but I was also pregnant. We looked at each other in silence until we both said it at the same time: "Wedding."

A lot had to change now that I knew I was pregnant. I had to get my dress altered because I was not able to wear heels anymore. I was no longer able to celebrate our wedding day by drinking alcohol. It was a bummer because I don't think I was ever at a wedding where the wedding party was *not* drinking. I was bummed and turned into even more of a bridezilla. My hormones were running amuck. In the long run, I knew what was important: the beginning of our happy little family.

***

Our wedding day was approaching, and it was getting down to the wire. Casey's parents drove up from Florida for the wedding. I was nervous. It was the first time that I was meeting them in person. I was more nervous and anxious than usual. I kept wondering, *What happens if they didn't like me?* Their son would have to live with a woman who they didn't approve of. Casey told me numerous times that if he loved me, that his parents would love me too. He is such a positive person and always brings light to the end of the tunnel, no matter how dark it is.

His parents finally arrived, and his mother welcomed me with open arms. She was so excited to meet Jaylynn and me. I can remember Casey telling me about his dad. He said that he was an ass and not to let that bother me. His dad was not very sociable with me at first, but as time went by, I believe that he truly grew to love Jaylynn and me. Casey helped me get a lot of things done to prepare for the wedding. We were in Syracuse using my dad's truck because we got our Chevy Malibu back, and it had a cracked window.

The day of the rehearsal had come, and we all met at Castaways Riverside Restaurant in Brewerton, New York. We had to finalize the decorations and have a run-through of the ceremony. I was so mad because it seemed as though my sister and I were the only people doing any work. I had 7 girls in my wedding party, and it seemed like nobody wanted to help me. My sister told me that I was hormonal because I was in the early stages of pregnancy. I didn't ever remember being hormonal with Jaylynn. She told me that everything would come together, and nobody would care about the small things. All my guests just care about watching Casey and I celebrate our love for each other. She was absolutely right.

I thought that I was going to have an anxiety attack, but my sister talked me down and said that the wedding would be perfect. I was thankful for her because she threw the most beautiful bridal shower ever imagined. She had small tree branches painted black with silver sparkles in a glass vase. It was so elegant. She is a firm believer in Pinterest, and that is where she got most of her ideas. I asked her if we could make the same centerpieces for the wedding because I absolutely loved it. She made things so special for me. I could never thank her enough.

It's wedding time! I didn't stay in the hotel the night before the wedding because I felt that since we were already married and I was pregnant, that it wouldn't be bad luck to see the bride before the wedding. I couldn't sleep the night before. I was in bed while all the men were downstairs getting drunk and playing catchphrase. I actually had to tell them all to be quiet because I could hear them laughing and being obnoxious. I did not get any sleep, and I had to be up early to get my hair done. The feeling of excitement was kicking in, but my nerves were on edge because I knew that this would be my first and last big wedding. I wanted it to be the best day for everyone. It was cloudy that morning, and I thought it was going to rain all day.

After Shannon, Jaylynn, and I got our hair done, we headed to my Mom and Dad's house to finish getting dressed. I was late. I arrived at my parents' house, and everyone that I thought was going to be there was there. I knew Billie Jo was going to meet us at Castaways. Mariah did my makeup, and some of the girls started doing shots and already had a couple of beers. I felt so bad that I could not toast with them and say cheers to my happiness. I did drink a sip or two of Pepsi just to get some energy.

I felt as though I was dragging, and I was anxious. We were joking around and reminiscing about all the crazy stuff we did when we were kids and adults, but we didn't go into too many details about that.

Gena finally arrived at the house to take pictures of me getting dressed. She laced up my corset and showed everyone how to do it so they can help while she was taking pictures. The one picture that comes to mind is the one of me standing by my mother's bedroom window looking down at my belly. It was beautiful knowing that today was a blessing and that Jaylynn and I finally had a great man in our lives. On top of that, she was about to be a big sister.

At that moment, I felt like I was finally getting my family and completed my circle in life. I kinda was in my own little world for a minute or two because I heard nothing but silence. Within that time frame, I took a trip back to memory lane. I remembered all the things that happened to me in the past, which reminded me of who I was and who I became. If it wasn't for all the hard times in my life, I wouldn't be the woman I am today. It was truly a blessing.

I returned from my daydreaming and heard my mom in the background telling me the limousine had arrived, and I needed to hurry up. We all piled in the limousine, and I start to get nauseous. It was not the greatest time to be getting sick. The girls were all taking pictures, drinking, and having fun while I was joking around trying to keep my food down.

When we finally arrived, all the men were walking in too. We had to wait for a minute until they all got inside. When we got out of the limousine, many people were walking in to get seated. My bridal party and I went to the dining area until the wedding started. It was at this point that I realized one of my bridesmaids was missing.

"Where's Billie Jo?" asked one of the girls. "She's not here."

"What do you mean she isn't here?" I asked.

I can remember that a couple of the girls tried calling her multiple times to see where she was at. Someone finally told me that she wasn't coming. I was in shock and disappointed, but the wedding had to go on. I had Nate Robinson and Joe Battles coming up to say me telling me that they were are about to start and we were not going to wait any longer for her to arrive.

Everyone was seated outside by the water waiting. My dad looked at me and said, "Let's go, and don't worry about it." I watched all my girls walk up before me, and I looked at my dad.

"I love you," he said as he touched my hand.

I will never forget that moment; it was hard to hold back the tears because I knew that I was his last daughter he was giving away. I knew it was the moment he had been waiting for all these years. I was so grateful to have found someone I love that loves me as my dad loves my mom.

Once I stepped out the door and looked around to see everyone that had come, my heart melted, knowing how many people loved us and our family. That is not all that touched my heart that day. It wasn't the fact that my husband and I wrote our own vows to each other, but he also wrote his own vows to my daughter, Jaylynn. He had spoken to Jodi, who married us the first time, and told her what his plan was for his vows. She made sure that she set time out just so he could recite his vows to Jaylynn. Most of the men were in their Dress Blues from the Army, and some were in tuxedos. Casey, along with all of his groomsmen, got down on one knee to say his vows to our daughter. That's when I knew she was not only my daughter but his too.

"Not only did you win over my heart," he said to Jaylynn, "but you also made me a father. I promise that I will always be there for you, and you will always be my daughter."

I, along with everyone at the ceremony, was crying. He gave her a ring with three hearts that represented all three of us in our new family. I knew that God blessed me with him for a reason. It was the best feeling—security. He made me feel so safe and relieved that Jaylynn and I had a great man in our life; we were finally a family.

I felt complete the day I married Casey in front of all our friends and family. I was excited that he was home from his deployment, safe and sound. I knew that we were going to have our challenges in life. We were about to have a baby, and we were still learning about each other. We were learning about ourselves, and sometimes our age difference did cause conflict.

We were extremely happy, and we were getting ready to announce at our wedding that we were adding a new member to our family. We were finally moving forward to our next big adventure together as a family. Little did we know that we were about to face some serious challenges together and miles in between.

Made in the USA
Middletown, DE
03 April 2022